HALAKHIC GUIDE

VOLUME I

CONCERNING THE JEWISH CALENDAR, FESTIVALS, AND SPECIAL DAYS

RABBI MOSHE SHAMAH

Halakhic Guide (Volume I): Halakhot Regarding the Jewish Calendar, Festivals, and Special Days

Published in the United States of America by
Sephardic Institute in collaboration with
Tebah Educational Services Inc.
New York, NY 10001.

A special thanks to Rabbi Ronald Barry of Sephardic Institute for his contribution to this publication with the articles "The Brooklyn Erub" and "Selihot".

For more information please contact Sephardic Institute at 511 Avenue R Brooklyn, New York 11223, (718) 998-8171, Fax: (718) 375-3263, email: info@judaic.org

Tebah Educational Services Inc.
by email at info@tebah.org.

Compiled by Norman E. Greenberg

Cover Artwork by Moses N. Sutton

Third Edition

ISBN 978-0-9792-5692-9

Table of Contents

Basic Structure of the Jewish Calendar

The Jewish calendar is based on both the lunar and solar cycles. Torah months are lunar and holidays are dated by the month. The holiday of Pesah is always to be in the spring month, that is to say the month of the Spring Equinox. Seasons are a function of the solar cycle. As lunar months are 29 days 12 hours 44 minutes and several seconds each, twelve lunar months comprise 354.37 days. A solar year is slightly more than 365.24 days. In just a few years of twelve lunar months each, Pesah would have drifted backwards relative to the seasons and occur in winter. To assure Pesah occurring in the spring, lunar months are intercalated (merged) with the solar year. It is the High Court's responsibility to intercalate as it sees fit. As it was halakhically established that a year be completely composed of whole months, the basic principle of intercalation was that an extra month is periodically added to the year to compensate for the difference between cycles.

Originally, intercalation was based on astronomical calculation and direct observation of the signs of spring. Early Talmudic sages checked the state of the crops and relied on the weather to determine if an adjustment (an extra month) had to be made in a particular year. As the primary purpose of adding the 'leap' month is to assure Pesah remaining in the Spring month, it is added just before Pesah's month (Nissan), and is called Adar II. By later Talmudic times intercalation was accomplished strictly by calculation.

It is also a halakhic imperative that months be composed of whole days only. Thus, the calendar is so structured that the 29 1/2 days of each lunar cycle are resolved into months of either twenty nine or thirty days each. In a 'regular' year (as explained below) six months have thirty days and six

1

months have twenty nine days. These 'full' and 'short' months rotate; Nissan is always thirty days, Iyar always twenty nine, Sivan always thirty, etc. Whenever a month has thirty days, two days are celebrated as Rosh Hodesh of the following month - the thirtieth of the outgoing month and the first of the new month. Whenever a month has twenty nine days, only one day is celebrated as Rosh Hodesh of the following month - the first of the month.

When a set calendar was established, intercalation was achieved by adding an extra thirty day month to the Jewish year seven times every nineteen years, as the number of days in 19 solar years is extremely close to the number of days in 235 lunar months, both comprising about 6939.6 days. Rounding out slightly:

365.2422 days per yr x 19 yrs = 6939.60 days

29.5305 days per mo x 235 months = 6939.67 days

An event's Hebrew date (luni-solar) and civil date (solar) will be very close to each other every nineteen years but not necessarily identical, as nineteen year cycles have varying internal patterns based on considerations which will be explained shortly.

In the calendar eventually settled upon, the seven extra months in each nineteen year cycle are added during years 3, 6, 8, 11, 14, 17 and 19. The set calendar was established by Hillel II, president of the Sanhedrin, in 359 C.E., based for the most part on the calculations of the third century sage Rab Adda. Basically, it is the calendar we have been using the past 16 centuries.

Additional calendrical considerations are that Yom Kippur not fall on Friday or Sunday (it would entail great difficulty having two consecutive days on which cooking, carrying, etc. would be prohibited), and that Hoshannah Rabbah not fall on Shabbat (which would interfere with *habatat araba*). This means that Rosh Hashanah, the first day of the year, cannot be set on Sunday, Wednesday or Friday. To accomplish this, one day is periodically added to or subtracted from the year. If added, it is always added to Heshvan (the month immediately following the New Year's month, Tishri); if subtracted, it is always subtracted from Kislev (the very next month). In 'regular' years, Heshvan has twenty nine and Kislev thirty days. In 'short' years, both have twenty nine days. In 'complete' years, both have thirty days.

As a result of the above, non-leap years have either 353, 354 or 355 days; leap years have either 383, 384 or 385 days. That the total days of a year be one of these six amounts became an imperative of the calendar. Altogether, encompassing exactly which days of the week the holidays of a year will occur and the number of days of that year, there are fourteen formats - seven for non-leap years and seven for leap years.

A problem is slowly developing. Rab Adda's solar year comprises 365 days 5 hours 55 minutes and 25 seconds. This measurement is about 6 minutes 39 seconds greater than the actual value of 365 days, 5 hours, 48 minutes and 46 seconds, which was not determined until centuries later. This 6 2/3 minutes annual 'lengthening' of the solar year adds up to about one day every 216 years, or about seven days since the third Century. This means that our average calendar dates have 'moved forward' seven days relative to astronomical reality as seasons have 'moved backward' by that amount relative to our calendar. The problem developing is that Pesah is slowly drifting away from the month in which the Spring Equinox occurs toward the second month of Spring.

The discrepancies involved in Tal Umatar and *Birkat Hahamah* are greater, as their settings are based on the less accurate calculations of Shemuel. This was explained in the study on Tal Umatar.

The originators of the calendar were undoubtedly aware that a slight discrepancy might exist. Just as their predecessors had corrected the solar-lunar calibration by direct observation, they expected the same would be done when the system would revert back to observation by witnesses or whenever necessary. It was always taken for granted that halakha was in harmony with reality. In the future, when a national Bet Din will be established, it will make an adjustment based on astronomical observation.

It is interesting to note that the Talmudic measurement for an average lunar month is strikingly close to our present-day measurement. It is claimed that the average Halakhic lunar month is greater than the true mean by less than half a second.

Halakha and The International Date Line: A Survery

I. The Problem

A prominent halakhic issue modern travel has posed may be described as follows: assume two people, starting from the same place at the same time, travel in opposite directions at the identical speed, one eastward and one westward. The one traveling eastward, against the sun's motion, would continuously change his time setting to a later time to reflect the fact that the "East" had the day sooner than the "West", as the sun always "travels" east to west. The westward traveler would continuously change his time setting to an earlier time, for the part of the day that had already been in the East is coming to the West - the West is "behind" the East. This phenomenon is reflected in the world's various time zones. When our two travelers meet at the exact opposite side of the earth from where they started, one would have adjusted his time setting forward 12 hours and the other 12 hours backward such that they both have the same time of day but consider it a different day of the week with a different date. Which day would be Shabbat for them? This question applies to all time-related mitzvot.

If our travelers continue in the same directions they had been traveling until they meet once again at the original starting point, the difference between them would be two days! Additionally, the one who traveled eastward would have a day and date one day earlier than the people living at the starting point and the one traveling westward a day and date one day later than them.

[As the sun "rotates" around the earth in 24 hours, and as the earth's circumference is almost 25,000 miles, the sun's movement at the equator is slightly swifter than 1,000 miles per hour. Somebody traveling westward at 1000 miles per hour would have the same time of day indefinitely, so how would he count days? What about space travel?]

The nations of the world addressed the basic problem in the 19th Century by establishing the International Date Line. Greenwich, England was chosen as the central point for time and date calculations, and exactly the other side of the world from Greenwich (180 degrees longitude or twelve hours) was set as the International Date Line. When passing this line traveling westward, one jumps a day forward, and when traveling eastward, one day backward.

A major consideration in setting Greenwich as the center was that the date line thus fell in the Pacific Ocean, preventing the inconvenience of its crossing large landmasses. In those few areas where it would traverse a landmass, where practical, the line was slightly bent; thus it is bent to go through the Bering Straits dividing Siberia and Alaska.

II. Proposed Halakhic Solutions

Most rabbinic authorities agree that logically there must be a halakhic date line that governs day and date for calendar-related matters but that it is not the International Date Line, as that was merely an arbitrary decision of the nations of the world which has no authoritative standing in Halakha. Exactly where the Halakhic International Date Line falls has been a matter of dispute.

One opinion reasons as follows: Jerusalem, the capital of the land given to the nation of Israel, is considered the center of the world for Torah purposes. From there, ideally, authoritative religious and ritual instruction emanates to the world. The Midrash teaches that we should consider Creation as having proceeded from there. Thus, the Halakha Date Line would be located at the exact opposite side of the world from Jerusalem - 180 longitudinal degrees away. In this way all the Jewish people, wherever they are located, would observe at least twelve hours of Shabbat simultaneously with Israel.

As Jerusalem is 35 longitudinal degrees east of Greenwich, the Halakha Date Line would be 35 longitudinal degrees east of the International Date Line, i.e., 145 longitudinal degrees west of Greenwich. When passing 145 degrees west of Greenwich traveling westward we change the date one complete day forward and when traveling eastward, one complete day backward.

According to this view, the only area affected by the Halakha Date Line being different from the International Date Line is that between 145 West and 180, for at 180 the rest of the world changes its date and everything is equalized. A relatively small number of landmasses lie in this "variance zone" of 35 longitudinal degrees, as it mostly spans Pacific Ocean areas. However, two important landmasses do fall in this area: Hawaii and a significant part of Alaska.

The complete string of Hawaiian Islands - longitude 154 W - 178 W - lies in this zone. According to this view the day called Friday by the Hawaiians is to be observed as Shabbat and the day they call Saturday is Sunday in halakha and requires tefillin, etc. *Mar'eet ayin* compounds the problem.

For well over a century, many observant Jewish residents of and travelers to Australia, Japan and other countries of the Orient have relied on this opinion, thus avoiding any difficulty associated with observing Shabbat on a day different than the local Saturday. They were careful upon traveling to Hawaii not to contradict themselves, where they would have to consider the local Friday to be Shabbat. Some people, because of the difficulty in observing Shabbat

7

on Friday and being concerned with the *mar'eet ayin* on Saturday, as the local Jews observed Shabbat on the civil Saturday, would leave Hawaii before Thursday night, which is Friday night according to their view. A difficult situation obtains with Anchorage, Alaska, a popular airline transit city, as it lies in the variance zone.

An important early work interpreted as propounding this view is *Yesod Olam*, written in 1310 by the Spanish rabbi and astronomer Isaac Israeli z"l, a student of the Rosh and the Tur. The famous English Sephardic rabbi, physician and astronomer David Nieto z"l, supported this view in his *Matteh Dan* (1714). One of the leading rabbinic authorities of the past century, Rabbi Yosef Eliyahu Henkin z"l, published a *p'saq* according to this view in 1925.

A different view is expressed in *Sefer HaKuzari* (ca. 1135), wherein Rabbi Yehudah Halevy z"l places the Halakha Date Line at the eastern tip of China. As the rabbi explains to the king, Israel is the center of the "inhabited" hemisphere, there being a quarter of the earth or six hours to its east and a quarter of the earth or six hours to its west. The other hemisphere, he explained, is considered "the other side" containing the "lands of the sea", regardless of the size of those "lands". The day begins from the East, or six hours east of Israel. The six hours of the west of Israel and the twelve hours of "the other side" complete the day. The Halakha Date Line is the spot where the day begins, 90 degrees east of Jerusalem.

Rabbi Zerahya Halevy z"l, another 12th Century Sephardic luminary, also arrives at this dateline in his *Ba'al Hamaor* Talmudic commentary. The Talmud states that a day may be declared Rosh Hodesh only if the new moon appeared in Israel by noon of that day, i.e., at least 6 hours before day's end (TB Rosh Hashanah 20b). This assures that there will be somewhere in the world that will have a full 24-hour day for Rosh Hodesh. (In days when establishment of the new month awaited proclamation of the Bet Din, which required sighting of the new moon, no place could have Rosh Hodesh before the proclamation.) He explains this to mean that the day begins 6 hours east of Jerusalem and the area just to its east are 24 hours behind it and 18 hours behind Jerusalem.

As Jerusalem's longitude is 35 degrees east of Greenwich, the Halakha Date Line according to this view is 125 degrees east. At Jerusalem's latitude - about 32 degrees north of the Equator - 125 degrees east is just a tiny bit east of the Asian coast, approximately at Shanghai's eastern tip.

According to this view, there is no variance between the International Date Line and the Halakha Date Line as far as Hawaii and Alaska are concerned - both are well west of both datelines. However, those countries east of China and west of the world's International Date Line would be in a "variance zone". In Japan, Shabbat should be observed on the day the country calls Sunday and the day it calls Saturday is halakhically Friday and tefillin must be donned.

The *Hazon Ish* z"l (d. 1953), one of the leading rabbis of the past century, was a vigorous advocate of this latter view. He interpreted it as based on the geographic knowledge that six hours (90 degrees) east of Jerusalem coincides exactly with the eastern edge of the major land mass Israel is located on. In addition, he posited from logic that the Halakha Date Line must take into account the unity of the contiguous land mass Israel is a part of. Thus, it is not only the 90 degrees that is critical but also the end of the landmass at Jerusalem's latitude. Accordingly, the complete land mass traversed by the Halakha Date Line would have the same day as their western, or Israel, side. Northeastern China, Korea, eastern Siberia and Australia would not be in what the other opinion considers a "variance zone" from the world's dateline notwithstanding that the Halakha Date Line passes through them or west of them; they are part of the land mass that extends west of the Date Line and are thus incorporated into the Israel timeframe.

The fact that 90 degrees east of Jerusalem does not precisely coincide with the eastern edge of the land mass Israel is on but is slightly to the east of it, entering a bit into the Pacific Ocean, is a question on this interpretation. The *Hazon Ish* proposes several solutions: perhaps the six hours or 90 degrees spoken of by the early rabbis was only an approximation, there not having been a need in previous times to be exact on this matter. Or perhaps in olden days the eastern edge of Asia at Jerusalem's latitude was exactly 90 degrees east but during the many intervening centuries the Pacific Ocean swallowed part of the land.

According to the *Hazon Ish*, the "variance zone" between the Halakha Date Line and the International Date Line includes Japan, New Zealand, New Guinea, the eastern Philippine Islands, eastern Indonesia, and numerous Pacific islands including those off Australia's central and eastern coasts. In these lands one would observe Shabbat on the day the local population calls

Sunday. *Hazon Ish* followers in Australia are careful not to travel to many nearby islands on Sunday as they enter into Shabbat.

Another opinion regarding the Halakha Date Line, held by some rabbinic authorities, places the halakhic dateline between the Bering Straits and Alaska. This opinion considers such a line as the "natural" dividing line of the world, separating the earth into two hemispheres. According to this view the Halakha Date Line is very close to the International Date Line and only some relatively minor Pacific islands fall into a "variance zone."

The International Date Line

Rabbi Menahem M. Kasher z"l (d. 1983, compiler of the 45 volume *Torah Shelemah* anthology), has written that in a matter such as this, which in his opinion (notwithstanding the above) has no clear tradition or Talmudic source, contemporary rabbis are free to set the line wherever they see fit and for everyone's convenience might as well choose the International Date Line. His opinion remains that of a minority of posqim.

Two prolific modern posqim have not written on the subject: Rabbi Moshe Feinstein z"l (d. 1986) and former Sephardic Chief Rabbi of Israel, Hakham Obadiah Yosef, *shlita*.

Former Sephardic Chief Rabbi of Israel Hakham Mordechi Eliyahu, *shlita*, ruled according to the opinion that bases the dateline 180 degrees from Jerusalem. He specifically stated: "this ruling is not merely to be *mahmir* (strict), but is to be followed even *lequla* (where it results in leniency).

Rabbi Ben Sion Aba Shaule z"l (Rosh Yeshivah of Porat Yosef) has written that one should consider this matter as unresolved between two major views and be strict on all Torah matters. According to him, in Japan, Hawaii and all locations that fall in the 90 longitudinal degrees that separate the two main views of the Halakha Date Line, one should refrain from work on Shabbat two days each week, fast two days Yom Kippur (eating less than a shiur to prevent danger to life), etc.

Others who also consider the matter unresolved with no established custom have (for the time being) deferred to the global following of the posqim involved and the difficulty of living without having a *p'saq* and allowed the public to follow either of the two major opinions but to be careful not to contradict themselves. Not to adhere to one *p'saq* when traveling to country A and an opposing *p'saq* when

11

traveling to country B. One who observes Shabbat on the local Saturday in Hawaii should observe Shabbat on the local Sunday when in Japan or New Zealand. One who observes Shabbat on the local Saturday in Japan, when in Hawaii should observe Shabbat on the local Friday. Travel plans must be made carefully.

III. Other Questions

Regardless of where the Halakha Date Line is drawn, how should one conduct regarding Shabbat upon crossing the line in mid-day? Should time-related halakha practice suddenly change on the spot or should there be a carry-over until the conclusion of the individual's 24-hour day? Although there has been much debate on this issue in recent generations, the majority today favors the view that the moment one crosses the Halakha Date Line, even if he remains on a moving boat or airplane, he becomes obligated in the halakha that applies to that spot exactly the same as one who lives on the ground at that location. This position is articulated in Rabbi Ben Sion Aba Shaule's responsa (1988, v.1 #14 p. 40):

I have seen later authorities who state that one who crossed in mid-Shabbat from the western part of the world to the eastern part of the world [traveling westward] where the day is Sunday, as long as he remains on the ship should continue observing Shabbat according to the time of the place he departed from. [Some say] even if he disembarked and reached a settled area he should continue observing Shabbat until the conclusion of 24 hours from the spot he departed from. Although many later authorities of our time are of the opinion that if he remained on the ship he should continue observing Shabbat according to the time of the place he departed from, it is my humble opinion that even while still on the ship or airplane, when he crosses

12

the Halakha Date Line it is permitted for him to end the Shabbat of the place from which he departed since he is now in a location where the day is Sunday and he is required to make habdalah in mid-day, skipping the berakha on fire. It sometimes may be that a person will have Shabbat for only an hour, when he was near the Halakha Date Line at the commencement of Shabbat and crosses an hour later. He would have prayed Shabbat arbit and made *qiddush* on wine and the next hour pray Saturday night arbit and make habdalah. He misses Shabbat shahrit, musaf and minha prayers. In the reverse, when he left the East Saturday night after praying arbit and making habdalah and an hour later finds he crossed the Halakha Date Line, he would once again pray all Shabbat prayers - arbit, shahrit, musaf and minha and make *qiddush* even if still in transit. We don't say he should conduct according to the place he departed from. Think about it - if two people left together, one from the East and one from the West, and they met - is it conceivable that one would have a halakha different than the other?

(Others claim that his rhetorical question at the end of the above quotation doesn't apply to the people on the boat, who only temporarily have a halakha different than the local island inhabitants from whom they are in any event separated.)

Rabbi Aba Shaule continues:

The same principle applies to weekdays regarding prayers. One who departed from the western part of the world to the eastern part of the world must recite the same prayer a second time [as he hasn't recited the new day's prayers] even though in his eyes it appears to be the same day.

Some authorities have questioned this position and advised in such cases to recite the amida "on condition", as follows: if obligated it is a regular prayer, otherwise it is a "nedaba" (a donation). As weekday prayers are essentially the same one day to the next and the individual prayed the appropriate prayer for the time-of-day period he is in, he fulfilled his responsibility for that day. The technical alteration of which day it is should not necessarily re-obligate him. This would not apply when one of the weekdays has a special character, such as Rosh Hodesh or Hanukah. In such cases the halakha would be similar to the case of Shabbat prayers, which follow the day's character.

When traversing the dateline traveling eastward, where the traveler "returns" to the previous day, there is almost a consensus that he need not repeat the previous day's prayer even though he is indeed in the previous day and will conduct in all halakhot as the previous day. Regarding prayer, he already recited the previous day's prayer. The same can be said for tefillin - he already donned tefillin for this day and date when fulfilling his previous day's obligation a short time before. However, regarding prohibitions arising from the nature of the day, such as Shabbat, he is obligated as on every Shabbat. (For mystical reasons only, Rabbi Aba Shaule advises that even regarding prayers in such cases to repeat the amida on condition.)

If someone missed counting the Omer a complete 24-hour day while located to the west of the Date Line and shortly thereafter is located to its east where it is the day he missed, should he now count with a berakha for the previously missed day? In the present location he didn't miss a day! The proper day for b'rit mila, pidyon haben, counting "seven clean days" and all day and date-related halakhot are affected.

The International Date Line

Those planning to cross the dateline should familiarize themselves with the details involved preferably by discussing the subject with a competent authority.

Selected Hilkhot Shabbat Guidelines

In recent generations, among the authorities our community has accepted were Hakham Matloub Abadi z"l (1889-1969), who was a rabbi in Aleppo before World War I and served the Brooklyn Syrian community for over fifty years and Chief Rabbi Jacob S. Kassin z"l (1900-1994), who was a rabbi in Jerusalem in his youth and led our community from 1933 until shortly before his passing away.

The numerous halakhic decisions of Rishon Lesion Hakham Obadiah Yosef, *sheyihye*, often coincide with the position of the aforementioned rabbis. It is advisable to be knowledgeable in his responsa. Most of the following collection comprises halakhot discussed in his works. Several are from the published volume of Hakham Matloub's responsa, *Magen Ba'adi* and several are straight from *Shulhan Arukh*. Sources are cited so that one may easily acquire additional details on each *p'saq*. As there may be qualifications and reservations, it is best to refer to the sources. Hakham Obadiah's *Yabiah' Omer* will be signified YO, *Yehave Da'at* YD, and *Livyat Hen* LH. Roman numerals denote volume, digits the response number. *Magen Ba'adi* will be MB.

In some of the following permitted cases, for various reasons, it may sometimes be advisable to *mahmir*, but not indiscriminately.

1. Soap and Toothpaste: It is permitted to use solid soap (YD II 50). It is permitted to brush one's teeth with toothpaste except if it definitely causes bleeding (YD IV 27).

2. Heating Food: One may heat fully-pre-cooked solid food even from the refrigerator by placement on a *blekh* (a metal

covering over the fire). This may apply even when there is a little liquid in the pot (YD II 45). (It should be noted that this remains a matter of controversy amongst the community rabbis.) Fully-pre-cooked liquids may be placed on the *blekh* to bring them to lukewarm if one is watching to make sure they will not be allowed to get hot to the extent of *yad soledet bo* (LH 51).

3. It is permitted to pour hot water from a *keli rishon* on coffee and sugar (YD II 44). One may pour hot water from *keli rishon* into a thermos container and cover it (LH 4).

4. Regarding use of a teabag on Shabbat. *Magen Ba`adi* #3 permits placing a teabag in *keli sheni* hot water while YO VII:40 only permits pouring hot water from a *keli sheni* unto a teabag but not placing the teabag straight into *keli sheni* hot water.

5. One may open a twist off soda bottle by separating cap from ring (YD II 42).

6. It is permitted to cut vegetables into small pieces for the upcoming meal. One may mash bananas or cooked vegetables (ready-to-eat items) with a fork to eat promptly (YD V 27).

7. It is permitted to break and eat biscuits or cake that has writing on it (LH 119).

8. One may open and close a book that has writing on its outer edges even though by doing so the appearance of writing is being eradicated and formed (LH 120).

9. When necessary, it is permitted to set a washer or dryer, etc., to operate before Shabbat even if it continues into Shabbat (YD III 18).

Selected Hilkhot Shabbat Guidlines

10. If necessary, one may give an item to a non-Jew for repair or cleaning (*bekablanut*, where he is not your employee) before Shabbat and pick it up after Shabbat even if there was not enough time for the non-Jew to do the job on *hol* – even in a Jewish neighborhood and with an item known to belong to a Jew (YD III 17).

11. One may place flowers in water even if they were not in water before Shabbat except if there are buds that would open (YD II 53).

12. Watches: One may wind a wristwatch that is running (wearing a self-winding watch) (YD II 48). One may wear a wristwatch into *reshut harabim* (YD III 23). It is permitted to reset the dial on regular (non-electronic) watches (YD II 48). One may wear an "electronic" watch that displays the time without having to press buttons. Pressing such buttons is prohibited (YD IV 49).

13. Women may use face powder, even colored powder (YD IV 28).

14. It is permitted to spray aerosol fragrance into the air and on one's skin, but not on clothing (YD IV 25). One may place fragrant spices in foods or drinks (LH 68).

15. One may spray pesticide in the vicinity of flies but not directly at them, provided a window is open for them to escape (YO III 20).

16. It is permitted to use diapers with adhesives in the normal manner (YD VI 24).

17. It is permitted to pin diapers or to pin an ornament to a garment (LH 121).

18. It is permitted to make ice (YD I 30).

19. One may squeeze a lemon even into an empty vessel (LH 57).

20. Damp clothing hanging on a line to dry at the beginning of Shabbat that are expected to dry by the next day are not *muqseh* and may be worn on Shabbat (LH 37).

21. One may knock on a door with a doorknocker (LH 111).

22. Grape juice is acceptable for *qiddush* (YD II 35). Soda, tea, coffee or milk are not acceptable even for habdalah or daytime *qiddush* (YD I 38).

23. Hadlaqat Nerot: The berakha should be recited before lighting the candles (the berakha does not imply *qabalat Shabbat* unless the person has such in mind) (YO II 16). Single girls do not light candles for Shabbat separately from their mothers – if they do, they cannot recite the berakha (YD II 32). If candles or oil are unavailable, the *mitzvah* may be fulfilled on an electric light bulb with berakha (YD V 24).

24. Women are obligated in habdalah (YD IV 27), *se`uda shelisheet* and *se`uda rebi`it* (YD IV 25).

25. Beginning at about six years old (depending on the boy), a boy who knows to Whom we bless may be given an aliya to the Torah on Shabbat morning, is counted toward the seven `olim and may read his own part. He may even be given maftir (YD IV 23).

26. We may offer ordinary transgressors `aliyot to the Torah and they can be counted into the required number of `olim (YD II 16).

The Brooklyn Erub

Commonly asked questions and answers regarding the Sephardic Brooklyn Community Mehisot Erub built in 2003 as authorized by the Sephardic Rabbinical Council.

The following responses were prepared by Rabbi Ronald Barry, summarizing the Sephardic Rabbinical Council's research and work on the Mehisot Erub.

What does an erub accomplish and what importance does it play in promoting Sabbath observance?

Carrying from one's home to an outdoor public area or vice versa, or within a public area is prohibited on the Sabbath. An erub is a halakhic solution for neighbors to pool resources permitting carrying outside their homes. It was applied to large sections of cities and towns and to entire cities. It helps to reduce hardship to observant families, the elderly, and the infirm as well as helping to remove Sabbath desecration by the less observant.

The Torah prohibition of carrying on the Sabbath is a very serious one and transgression of it by the general public is not uncommon. Traditionally the rabbinic position has always been that saving people from such a serious sin with a halakhically acceptable erub overrides all other considerations. Sabbath observance is the foundation of Jewish belief, practice, continuity and redemption. Creating institutions such as an erub to facilitate Sabbath observance is of the highest importance.

How ancient is the tradition of creating erubin and how mainstream is it to Judaism?

The Talmud relates a story way back to King Solomon that upon the establishment of the concept of erubin, Hashem responded with encouragement and praise. *Geonim* and *Rishonim* following the Talmudic tradition required localities to establish and maintain an erub even to the extent of threatening opponents with excommunication, as exemplified by the famous story of Rabbenu Asher in early 14th century Spain.

Throughout the past 2 millennia numerous erubin for towns and sections of cities are documented, both in the Ashkenazic and Sephardic communities. Today there are erubin for entire cities and neighborhoods throughout Israel and the Diaspora. There are perhaps 100 erubin in American cities and many in very large cities. Also, there are many in the planning stages.

What are the requirements for building an erub in a modern city?

Requirements for an erub in application to a modern city include:
- (1) determining that the area is not a Biblical public domain,
- (2) physically enclosing the area with walls and doorways,
- (3) acquiring the area from municipal authorities for erub purposes,
- (4) pooling resources together via a shared food item, and
- (5) no unenclosed disqualifying area within the boundaries.

What methods of enclosure are effective for an erub?

The classical enclosure is that of a walled city. Our Sages have also considered doorway openings - *Surat Hapetah* to be walls if they have two side posts and a string (any minimal lintel) that crosses directly above the top of the side posts. When the majority of a long wall is the *Surat Hapetah* (doorway opening format) type, some hold that it is not as acceptable. The more acceptable type has the majority of its length as a solid wall.

How many walls are required to make an Erub enclosure that meets even the strict view and removes any question of Biblical prohibition?

An enclosure that removes any Biblical prohibition, is called a "Mehisot Erub". It includes three walls with (1) the majority of each wall being an actual wall, (2) the minority may be a *Surat Hapetah* (poles and strings) wall while the fourth side may be entirely a *Surat Hapetah* (poles and strings) wall.

What is the legal definition of a public domain and how must an area be enclosed to convert it to be considered a private domain and allow carrying?

Shulhan Arukh states two different definitions of what constitutes *Reshut Harabim* - a public domain – where carrying on Shabbat is Biblically prohibited.

The first opinion defines a *Reshut Harabim* (public domain) to be streets that have all of the following conditions, and if it lacks one condition an Erub can be effective to permit carrying.
(1) 16 *amot* or more wide (24+ feet),
(2) no roof above it,
(3) no wall around it, and

(4) *Mefulash* – the street runs in a straight line from gate to gate:

> (a) even if it is enclosed with a wall if the street runs straight (*Mefulash*) from gate to gate the gates must be closed at night,
>
> (b) and some say that even if the gates are not actually closed at night but are capable of being closed (not permanently sunk into the ground).

Under this definition for an erub to be effective for a city with wide streets you would need either (a) walls around the city and gates at the entrances, or (b) the street endings do not run in a straight line (*Mefulash*), then walls around the city without gates would suffice.

The second opinion in Shulhan Arukh states: "Some say that any street in which 600,000 people do not pass through every day is not a Biblical public domain." This would preclude almost any street or city from being a public domain and remove a major problem for erubin planners. Most Ashkenazic rabbis and many Sephardic rabbis relied upon this opinion to construct erubin even in cities with wide streets that are straight (*Mefulash*) from opening to opening.

Which of the two opinions do we follow as the Halakha?

Normally when Shulhan Arukh has a "general" opinion followed by one of "some say" the Halakha would go like the first opinion. But since elsewhere in Shulhan Arukh the second opinion "that nowadays there is no *Reshut Harabim*" is stated and used as a possible explanation, it may indicate that the Shulhan Arukh is going like the second opinion. As a result we have a controversy in interpretation, with most posqim going by the second opinion. We must note that, due to this question, a significant segment of Sephardic posqim prescribe for Bnei

Torah not to personally carry within an erub that only meets the secondary opinion's criteria if also relying on another leniency where the walls are the *Surat Hapetah* (poles and strings) type. Wives and family of Bnei Torah are commonly not mandated to be stringent.

Are we permitted to carry without any type of wall enclosure if the area lacks one of the factors of a Biblical Reshut Harabim (public domain)?

No, as there is a Rabbinic prohibition on carrying in a "Karmelit" which is an area that is missing qualifications of a Biblical *Reshut Harabim* (public domain). In order to be considered a private domain in which carrying is permitted all five of the requirements of an erub for a modern city (listed above) must be met including a wall enclosure.

What is this Mehisot Erub that you have built for our Brooklyn neighborhoods?

Our Mehisot Erub is the preferred type of enclosure that meets even the strict view and removes any questions of both Biblical and Rabbinic prohibitions. The vast majority of 3 sides being actual walls and the minority being *Surat Hapetah* (poles and strings), with the fourth side being mostly *Surat Hapetah* (poles and strings). Due to the fact that our Brooklyn streets endings do not meet the definition of *Mefulash* and do not run in a straight line, gates closed at night are not required. As an enhancement we have added *Delatot* (gates) that are closed on occasion.

(For the scholarly reasoning of this approach, the following elucidates the details of this ruling. Brooklyn streets, although wide, are lacking any main street that goes straight from one end of town to the other end without a detour or significant curve. Also no street connects straight through from one town to another town since Brooklyn is

24

surrounded by water on 3 sides. This meets the straightforward definition of Maran Bet Yosef of not being "*Mefulash*", which then makes a Mehisot enclosure effective without necessitating gates closed every night. Even the section of Ocean Parkway that is within our erub borders curves sufficiently at Avenue W to be considered not *Mefulash* according to the writings of Porat Yosef Rosh Yeshiva Rabbi BenSion Abba Shaul Z"L. It is clear that according to our Sephardic posqim our streets are not *Mefulash* and, along with our Mehisot, remove any question of being a public domain. Maran Bet Yosef clearly states that if it is not *Mefulash* even only on one side, then *Delatot* (gates) closed at night are not required. As an enhancement we have added *Delatot* that are closed on occasion.)

Why do you call it a Bet Yosef Mehisot Erub?

Although the majority of the posqim have approved erubin whose perimeter is entirely *Surat Hapetah* (poles and strings) even in streets that are very wide, (see Rabbi Obadia Yosef's recent responsa permitting the Deal Erub and one in Los Angeles, Ca.) such as in Israel, Syria and Egypt, etc., we have taken steps to establish this erub with halakhic enhancements including that (1) the vast majority of the perimeter is made up of actual walls, (2) the gaps both larger and smaller than 10 *amot* are closed with *Surat Hapetah*, (3) gates are added.

Erubin experts who have studied our Mehisot Erub have declared it to be a "Bet Yosef Mehisot Erub", in which carrying is permitted even for our strict and G-d fearing members.

The Brooklyn Erub

Do our community rabbis endorse it and how reliable is this Mehisot Erub?

Our Sephardic Rabbinical Council members in 2003 unanimously deciding to embark upon this holy project for our Brooklyn community and after almost 6 years of research, planning and implementation, we proclaim that this Mehisot Erub has been built with the highest Halakhic standards for the members of our Syrian, Egyptian, Lebanese and other Sephardic communities in our Brooklyn neighborhoods.

We received permission from the appropriate authorities and have been granted the domain from the city as prescribed in the laws of erubin. Erub communal matzot have been officially designated on behalf of the entire Jewish community.

We have consulted with former and current Sephardic chief rabbis in Israel, and have received their blessings and halakhic approval of our efforts to build an erub for our Brooklyn Sephardic community, - some given verbally, some in letter format and in addition some referring to their supportive writings on the subject. Some have been posted on our erub website www.erub.org.

Subsequently Rabbi Obadia Yosef has written a letter to us in support of the Brooklyn erub and that one may halakhically rely on it and even for Sepharadim following the opinion of Maran in Shulhan Arukh. The actual construction of our Mehisot Erub has been constructed under rabbinic supervision of experts in the field of erubin.

What upkeep and maintenance will be provided to ensure the erub's continuity?

The *Sephardic Brooklyn Community Erub, Ltd* has been founded to maintain the upkeep and ongoing supervision and checking of our Mehisot Erub. They have contracted for weekly checking by a group of eminent Talmidei Hachamim, well versed in the intricacies of The Laws of Erubin, and for maintenance of the erub when needed. As weather conditions and other natural and manmade problems may cause any erub to fail, and although any problem will be addressed and fixed promptly, it is possible that on occasion the Erub will be down. As such an *Erub hotline number 718-375-ERUB (718-375-3782)* has been established for members to call and confirm that the Erub is in force. A website, *www.erub.org* has been set up including weekly email notification to subscribers each Friday. We have worked assiduously for over five year since the erub was built and it has not been down even one Shabbat.

How is it possible to build an erub in a populous borough like Brooklyn?

The second opinion in Shulhan Arukh that a public domain has an additional requirement of having "600,000 people traveling on that street every day" was relied upon to be lenient in constructing *Surat Hapetah* Erubin (poles & strings) in cities with a wide main street that is *Mefulash* (straight). It is not a criterion for our Mehisot Erub which is effective according to the criterion of the first opinion in Shulhan Arukh, and which can assuredly be relied upon even for our strict and G-d fearing members.

The Mehisot type of erub has been established in certain other North American cities where they were able to accomplish it, such as Toronto, Canada, West Rogers Park,

The Brooklyn Erub

Chicago, San Fernando Valley, CA and the new Los Angeles Erub. Where you have three actual walls and with a minority portion of each that uses *Surat Hapetah* to close off any breaches, with the entire fourth side utilizing *Surat Hapetah*, it is acceptable even according to the stringent view.

How does the 1970's responsa of Rabbi Moshe Feinstein Z"L regarding Brooklyn apply to our Mehisot Erub for the Sephardic community?

As we stated in the previous answer, our Mehisot Erub meets the criterion of the first opinion in Maran Shulhan Arukh. The 600,000 view is the second opinion which was invoked to take the lenient approach in wide streets where a majority of actual walls was not possible. It should not, and does not, apply when we've met the higher standard of Shulhan Arukh's first and strict opinion of what constitutes a public domain and the strict view of what constitutes an enclosure. Actually Rabbi Moshe Feinstein Z"L writes that he initiated and approved an erub for Seagate, though it is part of Brooklyn, as it had actual fences on 3 sides and used *Surat Hapetah* for most of the 4th side and included gates.

Although it would not affect a Mehisot Erub, can you explain further about the 600,000 opinion since it is invoked whenever an erub is planned, especially in Brooklyn?

It is important to clarify and correct what the masses have heard about the second opinion of 600,000 in Maran Shulhan Arukh which standard Ashkenazic Halakha relies upon. A goodly number of Sephardic Poskim also rely upon this – some straightaway and some as a Safek (doubt) within the two opinions in Maran Shulhan Arukh. Rabbi Obadia Yosef is poseq that Sepharadim as well may straightaway rely on this view without concern. Maran's

28

definition here of a public domain is precise, while the stringencies of some Ashkenazic posqim including Rabbi Moshe Feinstein Z"L clearly depart from Maran's codified definition. Maran, speaking of the streets that are defined as a public domain, states, "And some say that any (street) which 600,000 people do not traverse every day is not a *Reshut Harabim* (public domain)". Accordingly, a street must meet all 3 of the following conditions to be a *Reshut Harabim* (public domain):

(1) daily occurrence "every day",
(2) referring to a single main street, and
(3) involving 600,000 or more people in actuality, not just an assumption of 600,000 people.

Rabbi Moshe Feinstein Z"L's opinion on Brooklyn departs from Maran's standards by defining a *Reshut Harabim* (public domain) as:

(1) even an occasional occurrence and not requiring it to be a daily occurrence,
(2) combining together the entire population in all the streets of the city to make up the 600,000 people,
(3) even if 600,000 people being there is only an assumption, while in actuality it may be less.
(4) Additionally he counts people inside vehicles, which many posqim disagree with including Rabbi Obadia Yosef, *shlita*.

Nevertheless Rabbi Moshe Feinstein Z"L was lenient on erubin elsewhere, such as in Kew Garden Hills, Queens and Detroit, Michigan based on his reasoning that only in cities with close to 3 million people must you assume that there are 600,000 people in all the streets. He holds that this is similar to Israel's sojourn in the desert where 600,000 men are in the streets with about 5 times that number in the tents. At the time of his writing Rabbi Feinstein assumed 600,000 people in all the streets of Brooklyn because at the time there was a population of 2.7 million people. Plus, in those days there were thousands of visitors on summer weekends to Coney Island Beaches, bringing the assumed population in all Brooklyn streets to 600,000 on a hot summer day.

As much of his reasoning here and above was unconventional, he clearly stated more than once in his Teshubot that he did not make this a clear cut Pesaq for Brooklyn and only wrote down his opinion since there was a rumor that he was the Rabbi who gave the approval to the Flatbush Erub. It is interesting to note that it's common knowledge now that Brooklyn's census population decreased significantly from a high of about 2.75 million in the 1950's and 1960's to 2.3 million throughout 1980's and 1990's and 2.45 million in 2000.

Can you explain why our Sephardic Rabbinical Council rabbis decided in 2003 to make a Mehisot Erub, although our community rabbis of the previous generation did not, and may have not been in favor of doing so?

The problems involved with having no Mehisot Erub in Brooklyn have become greater, and the circumstances in our community have changed dramatically, enabling the building of a proper erub for our Brooklyn Sephardic community.

Several years ago our sister community in Deal NJ, serving the Brooklyn community for the summer and experiencing a similar situation with the identical population constructed an erub with the approval of our rabbis and the Sephardic Chief Rabbinate in Israel. Current and former Chief Rabbis, when visiting our community, observed for themselves the serious problem of carrying on Shabbat in our Sephardic Brooklyn and Deal communities and continuously urged the community rabbis to construct a proper Erub. The problem has become larger with the immigration from Syria ten years ago, as they had erubin in Syria, and people were used to carrying on Shabbat without restriction. In fact, many continue to do so here. Also, many more people got used to carrying in the summer with the Deal Erub and return to Brooklyn with confusion and great difficulty on Shabbat. Lastly, there are many people who traditionally keep much of Torah and mitzvot and are unable to abide by the prohibition of carrying on Shabbat. This fact was the compelling reason for the establishment of the concept of erubin in the first place by our wise Sages of old.

Our Sephardic community is expanding westward, with people purchasing homes and several major community institutions building in that area which is outside the borders of even the Flatbush (*Surat Hapetah*) Erub. People there are presented with major hardships for young families, the elderly and the infirm, and without any erub coverage upon which to rely even under extreme circumstances. Our Mehisot Erub borders will include that area as well and will alleviate this situation.

New Circumstances Enable Halakhically Approved Mehisot Erub

Our community rabbis of the previous generation may have been reluctant or unable to involve themselves in constructing an erub in Brooklyn due to worries and concerns that do not apply to our Mehisot Erub under present conditions. These include the difficulty in the past of getting permission from city authorities, doing the actual construction, and maintaining the erub. Today there are in existence numerous erubin built with city permission, including many here in various Brooklyn neighborhoods,

The Brooklyn Erub

with reliable Erubin Rabbinical experts and committees who on a weekly basis check and repair the erubin.

Actually, we heard independently from Mr. Sam Catton and Mr. Al Azar that their rabbi, Hakham Matloub Abadi Z"L, spent a year working on an erub for Brooklyn which he considered halachically doable with full knowledge of Rabbi Moshe Feinstein's opinion, but abandoned it due to circumstances out of his control. His reported writings on the subject are missing and therefore have not been published.

Another concern was that if an erub was built here at home in Brooklyn, family members would get used to carrying on Shabbat and would continue to carry when they go away to a city where there is no erub. Chief Rabbi Eliyahu Bakshi-Doron, *shlita*, in his Deal Erub *teshubah* with support from other major posqim, dismisses this concern. In brief, he writes that we may not add such new decrees. Additionally, as most of the places that our families go away to already have erubin that are relied upon to carry, such as Deal, Miami, and all Israeli cities, there should no longer be any such concern. Today we can count hundreds of erubin in cities around the world.

On a sociological level, our rabbis were battling much more serious matters that threatened the future of our community, in addition to the myriad of communal concerns the rabbis had in administering to an entire community. The concern for an erub was dwarfed by major community survival issues such as intermarriage, unity as a community, working on Shabbat by a majority of the community who were in retail businesses, or working for American companies with a six day workweek that included Saturdays with no Sunday substitution option. Under those circumstances with a lesser Torah educated populace an erub may very well have frustrated the rabbis efforts to increase Shemirat Shabbat

32

with some misusing the erub to work on Shabbat. It is understandable for our Rabbis to strive for the greater issues that would ensure our future as a Jewish community and they were extremely successful in their approach as witnessed by what our community is today.

And finally some of our previous generation rabbis may have been reluctant to rely upon an erub that is entirely made up of *Surat Hapetah* (poles and strings). Our Mehitsot Erub is being constructed with actual walls or fences for the overwhelming majority of its perimeter, and as such there no longer exist grounds for opposition based on this point.

There has been opposition to the Erub. Is active opposition to establishing a Mehisot Erub for our Brooklyn Sephardic Community justifiable?

We can learn from a very revealing responsa of the greatness of Rabbi Moshe Feinstein Z"L, who had halachically disapproved of the Manhattan Erub. He was asked if it should be opposed and protested against.

His response was that, although it may create confusion for some, he wrote that it is not for us to protest those who are lenient, and it will be permitted to carry there according to certain opinions. He repeated that those rabbis who established it are also great and capable rabbis, who have determined that an erub is appropriate and halachically effective and as such, we may not protest it. As such a Brooklyn erub which he never even joined in prohibiting should surely not be protested .

Chief Rabbi Jacob S. Kassin zs"l never recognized a *taqana* for the Sephardic community prohibiting having any type of erub in Brooklyn. He was personally against making an erub for various reasons and in 1934 joined an Ashkenazic group of rabbis expressing opposition. When people asked him about it he gave his reasons, such as it might not be a good enough erub, fear that there wouldn't be good enough supervision, that if it breaks down it wouldn't be fixed in a timely fashion, how would the public be notified and that when people get accustomed to it they might then carry in New Jersey. Never once was he heard to say that there was a regular *taqana*. When Hacham Matloub Abadi zs"l began work on a Brooklyn erub in the 1950s, Rabbi Kassin didn't cooperate because of his reasons, but he never denied the group the right to proceed. This has been well attested by many including Mr. Sam Catton, *shlita*

Furthermore, the erub our late Chief Rabbi Jacob S. Kassin zs"l opposed was one mostly of *Surat Hapetah*. His son Chief Rabbi Saul J. Kassin *shlita*, was very close to his father and knew his thinking better than anyone else. He has initiated this Mehisot Erub under present conditions that are far different than could previously have been imagined, as was pointed out above and is confident that his father would fully agree.

The hallmark of Chief Rabbi Jacob Kassin zs"l was his ways in fostering harmony and unity in the community. With all this in mind it would be blasphemous to his legacy to invoke his name in a protest against his own son initiating a major community service alleviating hardship to the elderly, infirm and families (especially our young mothers) with young children.

Protestors of our erub ignore the fact that many prominent rabbis including several former Sephardic chief rabbis of Israel have encouraged Brooklyn rabbis to make an erub for our Sephardic Brooklyn community. On many occasions Rishon Lesion Hacham Obadiah Yosef *shlita* impressed on us the importance of a Brooklyn erub.

In addition we have shown above that our Mehisot Erub is being done with extra strictness to appeal even to the very strict and G-d fearing members of our community.

What are the guidelines for our community as to what is permitted to carry?

One may carry within the erub only those items that are permitted to be carried within a private domain.. The main purpose of establishing the erub was so that one may carry within it house keys, tissues, handkerchief, eyeglasses, talet, siddur and other Torah books, food-items, other permitted items needed for Shabbat, push a wheelchair, and wheel a baby carriage.

Anything prohibited on yom tob would be prohibited on Shabbat within an erub. Muqseh items remain muqseh. Thus it is prohibited to carry or use the following: money, wallets, purses, pocketbooks, electrical appliances, writing implements, umbrellas, gardening and building tools, business and car keys, outgoing mail, cell phones, pdas etc., etc. Although there was never a specific prohibition of bicycle riding on yom tob or on Shabbat within an erub as stated by Hakham Obadia Yosef in *Livyat Hen* (#107), it is advisable to be stringent not to ride a bicycle unless for a misvah purpose.

No prohibited category of melakha on Shabbat besides carrying is permitted by the erub. Outdoor activities that violate the spirit of Shabbat remain prohibited, such as certain adult sports activities.

It is our fervent prayer that the Al-mighty bless this holy endeavor with success and that it be a source of great blessing to our community and K'lal Yisrael.

The Brooklyn Erub

The Shabbat experience for our community changed for the better these past 5 ½ years

This past 5 and a half years we have joined the ranks of concerned and capable rabbinic and lay leaders, who for millennia have established erubin in Jewish communities throughout the world. Thousands of community people have benefited by the erub. It has reduced hardship to observant families, the elderly, and the infirm, as well as helping to remove Sabbath desecration by the less observant. Even for those who choose to be extra strict, our erub impacts numerous Shabbat laws and situations in a positive way.

Sabbath observance, which is the foundation of Jewish belief, practice, continuity and redemption, has thus been advanced in our community. Using the erub, families of all ages, the elderly, and the infirmed, have enhanced their joy and spirit of Shabbat. Use of the erub has by and large not led to Sabbath desecration or any significant lessening of the Shabbat spirit, but rather enhanced Shabbat observance.

Halakhot of Yom Tob

I. Overview

The Torah prescribes six days of *yamim tobim* ("good days," festivals) in the course of a year:

* The first day of Pesah, Nissan 15
* The seventh day of Pesah, Nissan 21
* Shabu`ot, Sivan 6
* Rosh Hashanah, Tishri 1
* The first day of Sukkot, Tishri 15
* Shemini Asseret, the eighth day from the first day of Sukkot, Tishri 22.

Yom Kippur (Tishri 10) is not counted amongst *yamim tobim* as it is not a celebratory day.

Each yom tob commemorates and celebrates a different feature of the nation of Israel's history and its relationship with G-d. Pesah commemorates G-d's redemption of the Israelites from bondage and the Exodus from Egypt; Shabu`ot corresponds with G-d's revelation on Mount Sinai and establishment of the Covenant between Him and Israel; Rosh Hashanah (beginning of the new year) marks Divine kingship and human accountability; Sukkot recalls G-d's protection and providence over Israel.

In the Diaspora there are twelve yamim tobim each year: the first two and last two days of Pesah, two days of Shabu`ot, two days of Rosh Hashanah, the first two days of Sukkot and two days of Shemini Asseret.

The reason each yom tob is celebrated for two days in the Diaspora follows. In Mishnaic times the Israelites did not use a fixed calendar; rather, the *bet din hagadol* (the High

37

Court) awaited witnesses to testify that they saw the new moon and then declared *rosh hodesh* (the advent of the new month) accordingly. In this manner the dates for the upcoming festivals were set. In lands outside Israel there often was a doubt as to which of two possible days was declared the first of the month. This problem was a result of the fact that the lunar cycle is always approximately 29 1/2 days and it was possible that the first of the month could have been established on either of two possible days. (If witnesses did not arrive when expected, rosh hodesh was declared on the next day.) Because of the limited communications of the times, the doubt outside Israel was not always resolved by the time the festival arrived; in order to preserve the sanctity of the festivals, two days were observed for each.

In later Talmudic times, when a fixed calendar was used and there was no doubt as to when the first of the month occurred, the two day observance was retained out of concern that things may return to their previous state. Although modern communications renders the problem of the doubt inconceivable, legislation that was decreed by the High Court (Sanhedrin) cannot be annulled without the reconvening of another High Court, which has not been done these many centuries. Hopefully, we will merit its speedy reestablishment.

II. Prohibited and Permitted Work and Activities

Work and activities that are prohibited on Shabbat, whether from the Torah or by rabbinic enactment, are prohibited on yom tob, with certain major exceptions. Thus, writing, building, shearing, sewing, weaving, buying and selling, etc., are prohibited. However, the Torah permitted work of *okhel nefesh* on yom tob, that is, work that is performed for the purpose of eating on the day. Thus, kneading, baking, cooking, slaughtering and salting meat, are permitted.

Actions that are part of the overall system of *okhel nefesh*, but which are not generally done for the purpose of eating on the day they are performed, such as harvesting, threshing, grinding and hunting, are prohibited.

Using fire and carrying from domain to domain are permitted. Since these are so pervasively intertwined with *okhel nefesh* they are permitted in and of themselves, even if not specifically done for eating, provided they are done for some benefit that will be derived during the day. Thus, heating water (opening the hot water faucet) to wash one's face, arms and legs is permitted. Heating water to wash the whole body at once, such as in the case of a shower, involves a technical question and should be limited to the second day only (when it is not Shabbat).

Generating a new fire, however, is prohibited, even if done for the purpose of preparing food. The permissibility of using fire requires a pre-existing fire. This halakha is clear from the Talmud, Rambam and Shulhan Arukh. Rishon Lesion Hakham Obadiah Yosef writes that this prohibition includes striking a match. He acknowledges that several rabbis of stature in recent past generations considered a match as equivalent to extending a fire as it was deemed to contain fire in its tip. However, he states that this is not the view of the overwhelming majority of leading rabbis and that those accustomed to striking matches on yom tob should discontinue doing so.

One may turn on a gas range that has a pilot light as this does not involve generating a new fire but extending an extant fire. Many new gas ranges create a new fire when turned on and are the equivalent of striking a match, thus necessitating leaving a small flame on from before yom tob if one is interested in using it on the festival. If a non-Jewish housekeeper kindles a gas range for her personal use, she may be asked to leave it on.

Riding a bicycle (that is in good condition), roller skating, wheeling a carriage and playing ball are permitted on yom tob. Of course, if something breaks it is prohibited to repair it on yom tob.

Muqseh applies to yom tob as to Shabbat; thus, although carrying is permitted on yom tob, carrying money or moving it, etc., is prohibited.

Cooking on one day of yom tob for the next day, whether the next day is a weekday, another yom tob or Shabbat, is prohibited. This applies to all permissible *melakhot* of yom tob. However, it is permitted to cook during the day for the upcoming evening meal if the meal will be started before nightfall. (This is common on Shabu`ot when many congregations pray arbit of the second day early). It is also permitted to cook dishes that children may partake of before sundown even if the majority of those dishes will be served at night.

When yom tob falls out on Friday, it is necessary to prepare an *erub tabshilin* from before yom tob to permit cooking on Friday for Shabbat. The erub, comprising a cooked item such as a hard-boiled egg, and customarily a baked item such as a loaf of bread or matzah, is designated to be part of the Shabbat meal; thus, preparation for the Shabbat meal is considered to have begun before the onset of yom tob and in such a case the rabbis did not apply their prohibition of preparing for Shabbat. A berakha *"Al Misvat Erub"* is recited. The erub should not be eaten before Shabbat, and surely not before the conclusion of cooking on Friday for

Shabbat; preferably, it should be part of the Shabbat meals, making *hamosi* on the loaf of bread. When yom tob falls on Thursday and Friday, the erub only permits cooking on Friday for Shabbat.

Although today we use a fixed calendar and know that the first day of yom tob is the actual day of the festival according to the Torah and the second day is from rabbinical enactment, both days are treated equally except for the following few exceptions.

1. It is permitted to engage in burying the dead on the second day, performing all the work that is necessary.

2. The rabbinic prohibitions associated with *refu'ah* (therapeutic practices and medications) that are applicable on Shabbat for someone who is not in a life-threatening condition do not apply to the second day of yom tob.

3. In accordance with the famous rule that governs doubtful issues in halakha, doubts in halakha concerning matters of the first day are generally resolved strictly while those of the second day are resolved leniently.

The first two exceptions do not apply to the two days of Rosh Hashanah.

III. Candle Lighting, Qiddush and Habdalah

Candles (or oil lamps) are lit for yom tob, customarily by the woman of the home just as is the case for Shabbat; the berakha is '*Lehadlik Ner Shel Yom Tob*'. *Sheheheyanu* should generally not be recited with candle-lighting as it is expected to be recited in *qiddush*. If candles were not lit before sundown they may be lit in the evening, since the use of fire is permitted on yom tob.

41

The evening *qiddush* of yom tob begins with the berakha on wine, followed by a berakha that includes mention of the particular festival. If it is also Shabbat, the wording of the festival *qiddush* is recited with the mention of Shabbat included. Except for the last two nights of Pesah (which do not commemorate a "newly arrived" festival), *sheheheyanu* is also recited in the *qiddush*. On Sukkot, if one is eating in a sukkah, the blessing of *Lesheb BaSukkah* is attached to the *qiddush*.

When the festival falls on Saturday night, *qiddush* includes habdalah (in such a case making a distinction between "holy" and "less-holy"). The first two berakhot are recited as usual for the festival, followed by the berakha for fire (on a candle or oil lamp). Then the berakha of habdalah is recited. If it is a yom tob that requires *sheheheyanu*, it is recited fifth. Fragrant spices are not included in habdalah on a festival.

At the conclusion of yom tob, even between yom tob and hol hamo'ed (the intermediate days of Pesah and Sukkot), habdalah on wine is recited except when Shabbat immediately follows the conclusion of yom tob. In the latter case, only the standard Friday night *qiddush* is recited, for it would be inappropriate to mention the "departure" of yom tob in the *qiddush* for Shabbat. In the habdalah at the conclusion of yom tob only two berakhot are recited - on wine and the standard habdalah berakha that is recited on Saturday nights all year long.

IV. General Halakhot

It is a requirement to honor and enjoy yom tob. The Torah prescribes a special mitzvah to be joyous on the festival. One must make preparations for this purpose. Families eat together and guests are invited. In our happiness we are required to remember the lonely and needy and share our blessings with them. It is incumbent on all to make efforts to invite them to participate in our festive meals and to provide for their welfare.

Yom tob annuls the "*shib`ah*" for one who is "sitting" in mourning for a family member, including one sitting for father or mother. This applies only if the mourner sat at least a short time before the onset of the festival. Yom Kippur also annuls "*shib`ah*."

If someone passed away on the festival, the seven-day mourning period does not begin until after the conclusion of the complete festival, including hol hamo`ed. Until then, only restricted, private mourning is permitted. The second day of yom tob, when it concludes the festival, counts as day one since it is of rabbinical derivation and the individual did practice a degree of private mourning.

V. Prayers

In each amida of yom tob it is necessary to recite the portion that reflects the particular festival. If one mistakenly prayed a weekday amida without mentioning the holiday he must repeat the amida and recite the one for yom tob. Musaf is recited daily, including during hol hamo`ed. Tefillin are not donned on yom tob. A special psalm associated with the theme of the day is recited for each yom tob, evening and morning.

Hallel is recited on all yamim tobim except on Rosh Hashanah. On the first two days of Pesah, on Shabu`ot, and on all nine days of Sukkot-Shemini Asseret, it is complete Hallel with a berakha; on the later days of Pesah it is recited without a berakha.

Special portions are read from two *Sifre Torah*. On yamim tobim there are at least five `olim to the Torah plus maftir. The Torah is not read at minha (unless it happens to be Shabbat).

Ya`ale veyabo is recited in birkat hamazon. If one concluded birkat hamazon and realized he did not recite it, he does not repeat, except on the first night of Pesah and the first night of Sukkot in the sukkah, as on these two occasions the requirement to eat at least a *kazzayit* matzah on Pesah and a *kazzayit* bread in the sukkah on Sukkot is mandatory. If one realized he did not recite *ya`ale veyabo* after concluding the third berakha but before beginning the fourth, he should make the relevant insertion as found in the *mahzor*.

VI. Bicycle Riding on Yom Tob

The primary reason bicycle riding is prohibited on Shabbat is because it enters the category of carrying, moving an item from one domain to another or from one place to another in the public domain. This discussion is limited to yom tob when it's permitted to carry.

Riding itself does not involve any melakha. Exerting force on a pedal and through a mechanical connection moving or stopping the wheels is not a melakha of Shabbat. Halakha is full of examples of similar permitted devices. Consider exerting pressure on the lever of an aerosol container or a bathroom flush. Or winding a running watch. (We do not wind a stopped one because it might be considered "fixing" a "broken" item.)

The four usual halakhic issues raised regarding bicycle riding on yom tob follow. [Hakham Obadiah Yosef commented on them in *Livyat Hen* #107 (1986).]

<u>The first issue:</u>

Perhaps something on the bicycle will break and the rider will repair it. Repairing is surely prohibited.

Rabbi Yosef Hayim (The *Ben Ish Hai*) in *Rab Pealim* I:25 (1901), referring specifically to a bicycle, states:

> We should not make new gezerot based on our own opinions; it's sufficient if the people of these generations are careful with the gezerot explicitly specified by the rabbis [of the Talmud]. Therefore it is permitted [to ride the bicycle] in the Erub on Shabbat or on yom tob even if only for recreation.

In the Addenda, at the beginning of *Rab Pealim*, also referring specifically to a bicycle, he elaborates further:

> I have heard some say that we should forbid [the bicycle on Shabbat in the Erub] because it may break and the person may come to fix it. This is also a vain argument and unworthy of being stated. First of all, it is not so vulnerable to breaking. Furthermore, we should not make decrees that weren't made by the rabbis of the Talmud, for if we do there are numerous permitted items which are vulnerable to breakage which we would have to prohibit. We find in Shulhan Arukh Chapter 339 many things prohibited on Shabbat by the rabbis of the Talmud because one may come to write or fix and still we do not apply those gezerot from our own opinion to items not specifically mentioned by the rabbis. Thus, there are many cases where these gezerot that one may come to write or fix could pertain that are permitted because the rabbis did not apply this gezera to those cases.

See *Birke Yosef* [Rab Hida] on O.H. 339: "...'It is permitted to compose a song orally with poetic meter on Shabbat and we do not make a gezera against it that the person may come to write, because we only have what was specified by the rabbis of the Talmud.' This is simple and clear. Tosafot also wrote similarly...'We are not to compare the decrees of the rabbis one to another except where the Talmud compares.' See Sifte Cohen... and Magen Abraham... [who also say this.]"

Hakham Obadia Yosef cites this view of *Rab Pealim* favorably.

If a bicycle does break while away from home on yom tob, it is permitted to walk it home. A flat tire or disconnected chain does not render the bicycle *muqseh* as it is fit for some use even while in its dysfunctional state, namely, sitting upon.

Of course it is inadvisable to ride a bicycle on yom tob if the chain is not securely fastened. Such that it could be assumed it would not fall off that day.

The second issue:

Perhaps the rider will go beyond the *tehum* (2000 *amot* beyond the last house of the town) which is prohibited.

The same objection that we do not make our own gezerot these days applies here also. A further consideration is that the prohibition of *tehumim*, according to the accepted halakha, is rabbinic. The Talmudic rule that 'a gezera is not made on something which itself is a gezera' applies. This latter objection is also cited favorably by Hakham Obadia Yosef.

Additionally, in a large metropolitan area such as Brooklyn is, it is hardly ever the case that someone rides beyond the *tehum*.

The third issue:

Riding over an earthen surface may make a furrow in the ground that is considered in the category of digging, a prohibited melakha.

This issue is based on a gezera not to drag very heavy items over our fields for fear that we might 'dig' an agricultural furrow. However, a bicycle does not dig a furrow; the wheels press and pack the earth rather than dig into it. Furthermore, the rider has absolutely no intention to make a furrow in the ground. Even if a bicycle necessarily makes a furrow, thus cancelling out the lenient consideration of lack of intention, the rider does not care about it, especially as it is not a field standing for his agricultural cultivation. Where 'digging' is done in such an 'abnormal' manner (without shovel or spade), absent any intention for the digging and lacking any benefit from it, there surely is no prohibition.

These concepts are developed at some length by Hakham Obadia Yosef.

The fourth issue:

Bicycle riding is a weekday activity.

Most people in our community do not ride their bicycles primarily to shop or to do other types of work. A bicycle is ridden for pleasure, recreation, to visit family and friends, etc. Indeed, for many it takes the place of the automobile and is specifically used when the latter is prohibited.

Hakham Obadia Yosef did not think this question has much merit either.

Summary of the Basic Halakha

None of the questions raised against riding a bicycle on yom tob survive close scrutiny.

Kaf Hahayim, Rabbi Sassoon and Rabbi Obadia Yosef

The Kaf Hahayim O.H. 404:8 (c. 1906), upon citing the lenient opinion of *Rab Pealim* in some detail, tacitly indicating it as the standard accepted halakha, states that 'some' *posqim* were strict on this matter even though they knew that technically it was permitted. They obviously were making a gezera for their own local situation which they understood better than anyone else. Clearly the Kaf Hahayim is not citing 'some *posqim*' to indicate a universal gezera.

I asked the son of Rabbi S.D. Sassoon a"h what was his father's view on this matter. Following is Hakham Isaac Sassoon's response:

> In Letchworth we had an Erub around our yard and we asked our teacher, Hakham Yoseph Doury a"h, a wise, learned and reliable person, if we could ride our bicycles within the Erub on Shabbat. He told us that it is permitted providing we removed the horn and the batteries for the light before Shabbat. My father, a"h, agreed with him but was concerned with the feelings of the Ashkenazic neighbors who might not understand. So we refrained from riding on Shabbat.

Hakham Obadia Yosef, after demonstrating that none of the reasons to prohibit are adequate, states that it is proper to be strict because of the many rabbis that were strict. As he does not find any prohibition, and makes it clear that he decided this matter out of deference to the judgment of the majority of recent authors who published on this topic, community rabbis are not bound to modify established community custom (even if they may be inclined to do so in matters which he decides upon the actual substantive merits of the case).

The Custom In Our Brooklyn Community

There are many areas in which it is advisable to be strict. Sometimes the rabbis will establish a *taqana* or gezera; sometimes they will advise individuals that it is preferable to be strict privately. On the other hand, the Talmud and the great *posqim* throughout the centuries have pointed out that in many areas strictness may be counterproductive and have forcefully opposed strictness that is not clearly calculated to bring all-around benefit.

In our Brooklyn Syrian community the leading rabbis throughout the years have acknowledged that there is no prohibition riding a bicycle on yom tob. Chief Rabbi Jacob S. Kassin and others publicly quoted *Rab Pealim* on this many times. It is well known that a number of learned men, very particular in fulfilling mitzvot, permitted, and when necessary, encouraged, grown members of their families to ride bicycles on yom tob. Never did our community rabbis declare a gezera on this matter and neither did a prohibitive minhag arise.

Particularly in a community such as ours, where the rabbis worked long and hard to maintain great unity between the extremely religious and the moderately religious, it is inconceivable that they would have prohibited what was basically permitted when it would undoubtedly cause numerous families to be considered outside the law.

Our rabbis also worked long and hard to prevent the Conservative Movement from making inroads in our community. A major aspect of their success these past two generations has been their policy of not indiscriminately prohibiting what is basically permitted in areas that would make our people vulnerable to non-Orthodox enticement. Bicycle riding on yom tob falls into this category.

In cities where the extremely religious are separated from the non-religious in their social lives and where the threat from Conservatives has not been a major fear as it has been in the United States, it is much more likely that rabbis might consider a prohibitive gezera. At any rate we never heard our community rabbis during the past decades pronounce a prohibition on bicycle riding on yom tob.

Additional considerations not to prohibit what is permitted in cases such as bicycle riding on yom tob include the following:

* People inevitably discover the true halakha. This cannot be prevented. Some people may then be prompted to wrongly suspect that in other areas, where there really is an *issur*, the rabbis are not permitting what really is permitted. Some members of the public may become disenchanted with the rabbis, complaining 'why did not you trust us?' etc. To create the facade of an *issur* when there is not one is dishonest and sets a wrong example. If we want to make a gezera we should do so. There are rare cases when the situation requires that we not reveal the true halakha, but bicycle riding is not one of them.

Halakhot of Yom Tob

* There are situations where bicycles on yom tob serve an important *mitzvah* purpose. Consider the case of an elderly couple I know, whose children, very religious, live a forty minute walk away and never used to visit on yom tob. When they found out a bicycle is permitted on yom tob they began to visit every yom tob.

* The many teenagers and young adults who inevitably will ride their bicycles on yom tob should not feel they are doing an *issur* when they are not. Some of them feel they cannot help but ride their bicycles on yom tob and, psychologically, thinking that they are doing an *issur* may prompt them to doing a true *issur*. 'If I'm already doing a sin, what difference does it make if I commit another one?' It's a terrible way of looking at things, but unfortunately too common.

* As far as those who presently do not ride bicycles on yom tob, it's preferable they refrain from doing so knowing the halakha and choosing to be strict for their good reasons, rather than refraining out of a false concept of *issur*. In our society false concepts of halakha have fostered condescension and divisiveness, thus creating many problems. If, on the other hand, some of these people choose to ride bicycles on yom tob, we can assume they are doing so for good reason.

* As Rabbi Moshe Weinberger wrote in 'Keeping Up With The Katz's - The Chumra (stringency) Syndrome - An Halakhic Analysis' (Jewish Action, Rosh Hashana 5749):

> In our generation we have witnessed a miraculous renewal of interest in Judaism....However, we often encounter a somewhat questionable by-product of this renewed vigor, namely, halakhic enthusiasm which breeds halakhic competitiveness. This frequently results

51

in an overly restrictive, inaccurate version of Judaism replete with unfounded halakhic stringencies which may ironically deter others from seeking entrance into the majestic world of Torah Judaism. Often the 'pleasant ways of the Torah' seem to have become difficult to bear as a result of stringencies superimposed upon the truly pleasant ways of Torah Judaism.

Postscript

Although permitted, there are several considerations associated with bicycle riding on yom tob that may make it advisable for certain individuals to be strict for themselves or their families. Also, as stated above, it is inadvisable to ride those bicycles whose chains come off frequently.

Halakhot of Hol Hamo`ed

I. Overview

The intermediate days of Pesah and Sukkot, although not to the degree of the yamim tobim, are days of sanctity and happiness and are to be honored and observed accordingly. Families should get together, parents should take children on outings, students should visit their rabbis and schools should provide their students appropriate celebrations. The grand concepts commemorated by Pesah and Sukkot, namely, G-d's deliverance of the Israelites and His providence over them, respectively, are to be reinforced in the nation by all its members living a full week with the symbolism and procedures of these festivals.

II. General Halakhot of Hol Hamo`ed

Some types of work are permitted and some are prohibited. In general, factors that permit work are when it is to be done:

1. To prevent depreciation of capital or to take advantage of a passing opportunity.
2. For the purpose of celebrating the holiday.
3. By a worker who must earn income for immediate basic needs.
4. For a public need.
5. In an "amateur" manner.
6. For a therapeutic or medical purpose, even if not a life-threatening situation.

The economic system of the modern world has rendered many, if not most, business situations as involving depreciation of capital when one closes. There generally are many fixed costs that must be paid regardless of whether one is open or closed, such as rent, utilities, salaries and fringe benefits. This is especially the case for days of hol hamo`ed since they are attached to yamim tobim when it is mandatory to refrain from work. And in many cases other enterprises are dependent on one's business being open.

Men are to shave before the onset of yom tob for the honor of the festival. One who did not shave beforehand is not to shave on hol hamo`ed, even though shaving is a permitted labor on hol hamo`ed. This is a penalty the rabbis enacted to encourage all men to shave beforehand. One who did shave beforehand and in accordance with his regular schedule requires a shave every day or two, is permitted to shave during hol hamo`ed. In any event, one who shaved before yom tob and requires a shave before the last days of yom tob in order to enter that yom tob respectably, may shave on hol hamo`ed.

Haircuts are prohibited during hol hamo`ed.

The following activities that are prohibited on yom tob are permitted on hol hamo`ed: creating fire, use of electric and electronic devices, cutting nails, shining shoes, ironing, playing musical instruments, taking photographs and making recordings.

To assure that everybody cleans the clothing needed for the holiday beforehand, it is prohibited to wash and clean clothing during hol hamo`ed. This also provides the benefit that people do not have to spend valuable holiday time engaged in these chores. This prohibition includes giving clothing to a commercial cleaner during hol hamo`ed. However, it is permitted to wash and clean certain items during hol hamo`ed, particularly garments that soil easily, are washed frequently and are required for repeated use after short intervals. Baby garments are a good example of this.

Writing on hol hamo`ed is permitted when it involves something important that might be forgotten if not written. Students are permitted to take notes from the instructor for without notes they may forget the lesson they have learnt. Letters to a friend are permitted if they are not written or typed in a careful or "professional" manner.

III. Prayers

Ya`ale veyabo is recited in each amida. If omitted, and the individual did not realize it until after having concluded the amida, it is necessary to repeat the amida. If one realized the omission before concluding the amida he should return to *rese* and continue from there.

If one recited the yom tob amida instead of that of hol hamo`ed, he does not fulfill his obligation, since he did not recite all the required berakhot, and must repeat the amida. *Ya`ale veyabo* is recited in birkat hamazon.

Hallel is recited daily; during hol hamo`ed of Pesah it is said without a berakha but during hol hamo`ed of Sukkot with a berakha.

The Torah is read daily. Four olim are sent up on the weekdays of hol hamo`ed, the maftir reading from the sacrificial service associated with the festival. If a second Sefer Torah is available it should be prepared for the maftir.

Musaf of the holiday is said daily; it is the same musaf as said on yom tob with the word "tob" omitted.

The relevant mizmor for the festival is recited daily before arbit and after musaf.

Halakhot of Pesah

I. The Month of Nissan

Although in counting years we begin from Rosh Hashanah - the first of Tishri, the seventh month - the Torah counts months from Nissan, to highlight the Exodus from Egypt, which occurred in that month.

Since most of Nissan's days are festive occasions (the first twelve days commemorate the dedication of the Mishkan followed by Pesah), the whole month assumes a festive character; accordingly, *tahanun* supplications (ana) are omitted from prayers the entire month. The two Psalms normally recited in the latter portion of *shahrit* that allude to a 'day of distress' (*Ya'ancha* and *Tefila Ledavi*d) are also omitted when ana is omitted.

When one sees two blossoming fruit trees during Nissan, *Birkat Ha'ilanot* is recited. This berakha is recited only once each year by men and women. It may be recited on Shabbat or yom tob. Although Nissan is the proper time for it, it may be recited afterwards but not subsequent to the blossoming stage, when the fruit are growing.

Eulogies are not permitted during Nissan. When appropriate, a short appreciation of the departed with moral instruction is permitted.

II. Searching for Hametz

As the Torah prohibits possession of hametz on Pesah, it is mandatory to check one's home and remove all hametz before Pesah. Despite the fact that the home was thoroughly cleansed of hametz beforehand, on the night before Pesah we perform *bediqat hametz* in all places where it might be found. When Pesah falls on Saturday night, the search is done the Thursday night before.

Before beginning the search, the head of household (the leader of the search) recites the berakha *Asher qideshanu bemisvotav vesivanu `al bi'ur hametz* ("Who has sanctified us with his commandments, and commanded us on the removal of hametz"), which covers the entire process of the removal of hametz from ones property, completed the following morning; no berakha is recited upon the actual removal of the hametz in the morning. After the berakha, one must be careful not to speak until at least beginning the search, so as not interrupt between the berakha and the act for which the berakha was recited. It is proper to refrain from extraneous talk and digressions throughout the search so that it is done correctly. In addition to homes, places of business and cars require checking if hametz is normally brought into them.

Traditionally, the search has been performed by the light of a single wick candle (a multi-wick one is dangerous). Today, because of safety reasons and superior effectiveness in searching, a flashlight is preferable. A widespread custom is to use a candle for the first moments of the search for symbolic reasons and then switch to a flashlight. The berakha is recited even if one uses only a flashlight.

As the home is usually thoroughly cleansed from hametz before the *bediqah*, it is customary but not mandatory to place pieces of hametz where the searcher will surely find them so that he will have hametz to burn.

Immediately after the search at night, the owner should recite *Bitul Hames*, an annulment/renunciation of hametz in his possession. As most people will continue owning and

Halakhot of Pesah

benefiting from hametz until the morning, this first *bitul* is directed only to hametz that the owner does not know about. One should understand what he is saying. If one does not understand the traditional Aramaic words of the *bitul* formula (found at the beginning of the Hagaddah or Mahzor), he should recite it in English. Translations are readily available.

If one embarks on a journey within 30 days before Pesah and no one remains at home to do *bediqah* at the designated time, it should be done before leaving without reciting the berakha. When one closes his home prior to the evening of *bediqat hametz* and intends to be away the entire holiday, such as when a family goes out of town, if he sells any and all hametz in his home, he does not have to search it. He searches his hotel room and makes bitul for any hametz that may remain in his possession. The same applies to a second home that remains closed for the duration of the holiday. One who plans to leave the day of Ereb Pesah, since he is still at home at the time of *bediqat hametz*, is required to perform it.

One who was planning to be away all Pesah and sold the hametz in his home without making *bediqah* but unexpectedly returned must search for and gather the sold hametz that was not put away and place it in a closed off or out of the way location, to prevent someone inadvertently partaking of it.

III. Ereb Pesah

It is forbidden to eat hametz after the fourth hour of the day beginning from dawn. These hours are calculated according to a system whereby dawn to dusk is divided into twelve hours regardless of the actual length of that particular day (*sha`ot zemaniyot*/proportional hours). The time will vary

58

slightly each year according to the solar date on which Pesah occurs, but generally it is about 8:45 a.m. E.S.T. Consult the specific schedule for that year for exact times.

The prohibition to benefit from hametz, which includes selling it, begins one proportional hour after the deadline for eating, generally about 10:00 a.m. E.S.T.

It is preferable to completely get rid of all hametz without having to sell. However, selling is permitted even if the hametz remains in the overall confines of one's home, providing the hametz's specific location is also sold or leased to the non-Jew. As this transaction must be done legally, it is advisable for one who sells hametz that is going to remain in the overall confines of his property to do so through a rabbi. Hametz being sold should be gathered together, covered and placed where no member of the household would forget and mistakenly partake of it.

The destruction of any remaining hametz should be done before the end of the fifth hour. It may be accomplished either by burning, shredding, dissolving, etc. It is customary and preferable to destroy hametz through burning. When Ereb Pesah falls on Shabbat, the burning takes place on Friday.

Hametz in a garbage receptacle placed by the street curb in front of one's home is *hefker* (ownership is relinquished) and not in one's possession even if the sanitation department did not remove it by the end of the fifth hour. It is preferable that the hametz not be in one's private receptacle but in a carton or bag that will be collected with the hametz.

After getting rid of all hametz, one recites *Bitul Hames* again. This second recitation, unlike the night before,

59

includes all hametz one owns. Selling hametz to a non-Jew should be done before this bitul, since hametz being sold is not that which is being annulled or renounced.

Matzah should not be eaten Ereb Pesah even in the morning so as to eat the matzah of the Seder with greater desire and appetite. This applies only to matzah with which one may fulfill the obligation in the evening, not egg matzah which is called 'rich' matzah and is unsuitable for fulfilling the *mitzvah*.

Cake made with matzah meal, since it is baked the way bread or matzah is, should also not be eaten Ereb Pesah. Although the matzah meal was mixed with 'enriching' items, the mixing was done after the matzah received its identity as matzah fit for the mitzvah of the Seder, not at the original kneading like egg matzah. On the other hand, if the matzah is not baked but fried or cooked, such as *i'jeh masso*, it is permitted Ereb Pesah.

One should not eat a filling meal of any food in the later afternoon as it may lessen one's appetite for the evening's matzah.

There is a custom for first born males to fast Ereb Pesah as a sign of appreciation for the Almighty's sparing Israel's first-born when smiting the Egyptian first-born. This fast is overridden if the first-born participates in a *se`udat misvah* (festive meal attached to a mitzvah), including the completion of a tractate of the Talmud even though he himself has not learned that tractate.

IV. Shabbat Ereb Pesah (following times in New York)

1. The *Siyyum Bekhorot* is pushed back to Thursday and is treated more leniently than in other years. A non-bekhor

father who might normally attend a siyyum on behalf of his first born minor son is exempt, as are women *bekhorot*.

2. *Bediqat Hames* (searching for hametz) is done Thursday night after the stars appear (approximately 25 minutes after sunset) followed by recital of the first *Kal Hamirah* (annulling unseen hames).

3. Hametz is burned Friday morning by the end of the fifth hour (usually aproximately 10:10 a.m.), the same time as in other years so that there be one uniform halakha for all years, notwithstanding that this year we are permitted to eat and own hames until Shabbat morning.

4. The second *Kal Hamirah* (annulling all hames) is recited Shabbat morning by the end of the fifth hour (usually aproximately 10:10 a.m.).

5. Regarding *Hamosi* and Birkat Hamazon for the meals of Friday night and Shabbat day, several options are available:

A. We may eat bread (preferably pita which produces fewer crumbs) Friday night and Shabbat morning until the end of the fourth hour (usually approximately 8:55 a.m.), taking care not to have hametz spread over the house or fall on Pesah utensils. Only a minimal amount of hametz, that which is expected to be eaten, should be left for this purpose. Any leftover hametz must be discarded by 10:10 a.m., by which time the final *Kal Hamirah* is recited. Disposal of hametz should be into a garbage bag or receptacle left outside the home within the home's erub area (halakhic enclosure for purposes of carrying on Shabbat.) As a last resort hametz leftovers may be flushed away. This option generally involves attending first minyan that Shabbat morning.

B. One who chooses to remove all hametz on Friday, reciting the final *Kal Hamira* at that time, and uses regular matzah Friday night in place of bread, would recite *Hamosi* and Birkat Hamazon as during Pesah. For the Shabbat day meal, fried or cooked whole matzah, prepared from before Shabbat, may be used. The blessings on these items would be as during Pesah: *Hamosi* and Birkat Hamazon. Although we may not eat regular matzah on Ereb Pesah Shabbat during the daytime, fried or cooked matzah is allowed.

C. Egg Matzah is Mezonot unless one eats a large amount of it (at least 6 ounces), in which case *Hamosi* and Birkat Hamazon are recited.

V. Hametz

The Torah forbids eating, deriving benefit from, or owning hametz during Pesah.

Hametz results when any of the five grains (wheat, barley, rye, oats, spelt), after harvesting, makes contact with water and fermentation takes place. Mixtures including hametz are also prohibited as are edible extracts and alcoholic fermentation of hametz. Bread, cereal, cake, cookies, crackers, pastas and spaghetti from the five grains are pure hametz.

Rice, soy, corn (maize), potatoes, fruits, vegetables, meat, poultry, fish and dairy products are permitted when in their pure form. If processed, one must be careful that the product does not include or did not absorb from a hametz derivative.

Hametz derivatives unfit for human or animal consumption are not considered food and are permitted on Pesah. This includes virtually all deodorants, soaps, cleansers and cleaning agents, polishes, toothpastes, lipsticks, most cosmetics and medicines (all ill tasting liquids, tablets and capsules), etc.

Hametz mixed into non-hametz substances during Pesah is not annulled in the manner that prohibited food items are annulled all year long, such as mixtures of one in sixty. Perhaps more than any other, it is this halakha that requires an extra measure of care with food throughout Pesah.

However, hametz that was mixed with non-hametz is annulled before Pesah in the standard manner and remains annulled during Pesah. This principle applies even if inclusion of the hametz ingredient was not known before Pesah. Thus, foods prepared before Pesah that are known to be kosher all year long, that do not have hametz as an ingredient, even were they somehow to have a minor amount of hametz mixed in and annulled before Pesah, are acceptable during Pesah. Such foods do not necessarily require special supervision. Included in this category are canned, frozen and most dried fruits and vegetables, fruit juices, sugar, salt, plain tea, plain potato chips, pure coffees, pure chocolates, pure vegetable oils, tomato sauce, milk, butter and plain dairy products.

Based on this halakha, many homemakers bake, cook and purchase as much as possible of their Pesah needs before the onset of the holiday.

If hametz gets mixed into food even during Pesah, and gives a negative taste into the food, that food is permitted. Thus, if Pesah food was mistakenly cooked in clean non-Pesah utensils that weren't used for 24 hours, the food is permitted. This is based on the principle that whatever is absorbed in the walls of utensils gives a spoiled taste after 24 hours.

Ashkenazim eating by Sephardim during Passover need not be concerned that the vessels in which foods were prepared were also used for rice and legumes, which most Ashkenazim do not eat during Pesah. The Ashkenazic strictness on these items is an extreme cautionary measure and does not carry over to vessels.

One who finds hametz in his possession during hol hamo`ed should burn it immediately; if found on yom tob, however, it should be covered until after yom tob, at which time it should be burned. There is no berakha on these cases of burning.

Hametz be`ayin (roughly translated "visible," not a mixture) which was in the possession of a Jew during Pesah is prohibited even after Pesah.

VI. Matzah

It is a Biblical command to eat matzah (unleavened bread) on the first night of Pesah. It commemorates our ancestors not having time to allow their dough to leaven before baking, as they were chased out of Egypt. Also, matzah is the "bread of affliction," recalling the slavery.

Matzah is made from flour of one of the five types of grains that can become hametz, kneaded with water and baked before it has a chance to begin leavening (rising).

For this *mitzvah* one should obtain matzah that has been under supervision that it did not come into contact with water from the grain harvest. Each person should eat at least the *kazzayit* for *hamosi*, but preferably all matzah for the

Halakhot of Pesah

mitzvot required at the Seder, from such matzah. If not available, matzah under supervision from the grinding is sufficient. All commercial Passover matzah from the companies displaying supervision today has been "watched" at least from the time of grinding.

Matzah, once baked, may be dipped in water. An elderly or ill person may fulfill the *mitzvah* in such a manner.

Egg matzah is permitted to be eaten during Pesah. Indeed, matzah which was kneaded with fruit juice and not water, which is the standard procedure for making egg matzah, does not become hametz even if the dough was left unbaked for a lengthy period of time. (The acid does not permit activation of the leavening enzyme in the dough.) However, egg matzah is not "poor man's bread" and cannot be used to fulfill the obligations of the Seder.

The berakha on regular matzah during all of Pesah is *hamosi* even if one is eating a very small amount. During Pesah, matzah is our bread. Even when regular matzah is fried or cooked during Pesah, such as in *i'jeh masso* or *kibbeh masso*, its berakha is *hamosi*. All year long we recite mezonot on regular matzah except when one is *qobey`a se`uda* (there are various opinions here, essentially when one uses matzah to get full as bread) as matzah is normally a snack food in the category of a cracker. The berakha *Al Akhilat Masah* is added to *hamosi* only at the Seder. Egg matzah, even during Pesah, is mezonot (except if one is *qobey'a se`uda*).

VII. Utensils for Passover

Pesah requires special utensils to ensure that even a little hametz not enter our food.

65

Glassware does not absorb and merely requires washing to be kosher for Pesah. This includes Duralex, Pyrex, Corningware, Corelle and colored glass.

Absorption by utensils from food takes place in the presence of heat; thus, utensils that come into contact with foods and liquids that generally are not hot (salad bowls, fruit trays, refrigerator trays, can openers, etc.) can be used on Pesah after being washed. The same applies to tabletops and counters.

Utensils used with heat but known not to be used for hametz all year long are acceptable for Pesah, such as teapots, hot water urns and decanters.

Koshering utensils is according to its general use. As the utensil absorbed so will it emit what it absorbed. Hametz pots and pans, flatware, blenders, etc. made of metal, wood, rubber, stone, bone or plastic (including melmac and tupperware), can be made usable for Pesah by *hag`alah.*

Hag`alah is total submersion of the item being koshered into a large pot of boiling water for several seconds. If the item cannot fit completely into a large pot, it may be submersed portion by portion. The utensils must be cleaned before immersion.

If one is to make *hag`alah,* it is preferable to do so before Pesah. However, it can be made during hol hamo`ed providing the hametz utensil being cleaned was not used for 24 hours, based on the principle that whatever is absorbed in a utensil's walls emits a spoiled taste after 24 hours.

When *hag`alah* is made on items that had not been used for 24 hours in a pot that also had not been used for 24 hours, it does not matter if the items or pot are dairy or meat, or if the pot is hametz or kosher for Passover.

Metals used directly on the fire with hametz require *liboon* (placement on fire until red hot).

Utensils usually used for cold substances that on occasion were used for hot hametz, such as metal cold liquid drinking cups, are treated according to their usual use and merely require washing (after 24 hours from hametz use). Although the vessel on occasion definitely absorbed hametz, after 24 hours whatever was absorbed is spoiled; thus there is no possibility of a Torah infraction and the rabbis did not decree a prohibition when the usage with heat was not according to the vessel's standard usage.

Hametz earthenware utensils cannot be made usable for Passover. Glazed chinaware is very different from classic earthenware and many authorities permit koshering such utensils through *hag'alah* or pouring boiling water on them. An Orthodox rabbi should be consulted regarding the specific type of chinaware in question.

Porcelain, enamel and steel sinks are koshered by pouring boiling water all around their receptacle portion.

Ovens and their racks should be cleansed for Passover as follows: after thoroughly cleaning with a scouring agent, leave unused for 24 hours; then heat at maximum for an hour. Self cleaning ovens merely need to be run through a self cleaning cycle. In the case of microwave ovens, after cleaning, insert a microwave safe utensil with water and microwave at maximum for several minutes, until the oven fills with steam.

Dishwashers are koshered by their normal use of boiling water and soap.

Tablecloths are koshered by washing in soap and water.

VIII. The Seder

Qadesh After arranging the items on the Seder table correctly, the head of household recites *qiddush*. Everyone should be standing and attentive and there should be no talking during the recital of the berakhot. *Qiddush* is recited after *set hakokhabim* (the appearance of stars, which in New York is about 35 minutes after sunset).

Each person should have his or her own cup containing at least 3 ounces (*rebi'it*) of wine and drink at least the majority of the cup. Red wine is preferable but grape juice may be used. This is the first of the four Seder cups. These regulations apply to all four cups. The berakha of *hagefen* is recited on the first and third cups only. The drinking of the four cups and the eating of the matzot are done while reclining to the left. A left-handed person also reclines to the left.

Urhas Each person washes his or her hands for the wet vegetables going to be eaten next. A berakha is not recited on this washing of hands.

Karpas We eat less than a *kazzayit* of a green vegetable (celery is our custom) after dipping it in salt water. [The reason for having less than a *kazzayit* is to avoid a centuries old unresolved question: should one who eats a measure that requires berakha aharona of *Bore Nefashot* recite that berakha if he plans to shortly afterwards recite *hamosi* that will eventually be followed by Birkat

Hamazon? We try to avoid omitting a required berakha but not to recite an unrequired berakha.]

We recite *Boreh Peri Ha'adamah* on the karpas vegetable. It is our custom to have intention that this berakha "cover" the adamah of the maror, which will be eaten later. Although the maror will be eaten after *hamosi*, it is necessarily eaten alone and perhaps not covered by *hamosi*. So again, to avoid a question we cover it with the berakha on the karpas.

Yahas The middle matzah is broken, by hand, into two pieces. The smaller piece is replaced between the two whole matzot while the larger piece is set aside for Afiqoman. Each individual takes a turn carrying the afiqoman matzah, wrapped in a cloth holder, over one's shoulder reciting *Mish'arotam...* as a symbolic reenactment of the Exodus.

Magid One raises the matzah and recites *Ha Lahma `Anya*. The tray is removed for children to question, the second cup of wine is poured, *Ma Nishtana* is recited, the tray returned, and the matzot uncovered. The Haggadah is read with great joy. Questions are asked, explanations are given. The relating by fathers to sons of the Exodus from Egypt and the Almighty's miracles is the central theme of the Seder. Those who do not understand Hebrew must perform this *mitzvah* in a language they understand. English translations are readily available.

Rohsa One should wash his or her hands and recite the berakha *Al Netilat Yadayim* to prepare for *hamosi*.

Mosi Masah The head of the household raises all 3 matzot (the two whole and one broken) and recites the berakha of *hamosi*. Next, he releases the bottom whole matzah and recites the berakha of *Al Akhilat Masah*. Reclining to their

Halakhot of Pesah

left, all eat at least one *kazzayit* (approximately one ounce). It is preferable to eat two *kazzaytim*, one for *Mosi* and one for *Masah*. At least one *kazzayit* should be eaten within a four minute period to be considered a single eating.

Maror *Kazzayit* maror (bitter herbs) is dipped in haroset (a date, nut and wine mixture), the berakha *Al Akhilat Maror* is recited, and the maror is eaten without reclining. Romaine Lettuce is a preferred vegetable for maror but great care must be taken that it first be thoroughly checked and cleansed of any tiny insects that are often found in it. Escarole or endives are acceptable and generally easier to check.

Korekh A sandwich containing one *kazzayit* each of matzah and maror is dipped in haroset and eaten in a reclining position after reciting the explanation of this custom, *Zekher Lamiqdash* etc. Those for whom it is difficult to have *kazzayit* matzah and maror may eat smaller measures for korekh.

Shulhan Orekh The egg and shankbone are eaten followed by the meal. On the egg we recite *Zekher LeQorban Hagiga*. Nothing is recited on the shankbone. To distinguish from the Pesah sacrifice brought in the days of the Bet Hamiqdash which was only broiled, the shankbone should also be cooked. It is important not to be totally satiated during the meal in order to leave room for the afiqoman, which must be eaten "with appetite."

Safon After the meal a piece of the middle matzah is distributed to each person, to which additional matzah is added to make a *kazzayit*. This should be eaten reclining before midnight.

Barekh The third cup of wine is poured and Birkat Hamazon is recited.

Hallel Hagefen is recited before drinking the third cup, reclining. One should have intention to also cover the fourth cup with this berakha. The remainder of Hallel is recited without a berakha beforehand, followed by Nishmat and the concluding berakha of Hallel. The fourth cup is drunk, reclining, followed by berakha aharona.

Nirsa It is customary to sing and continue discussion of the Exodus and other miracles that the Almighty wrought until one falls asleep.

IX. Measurements

The measure for a *kazzayit* matzah is thought by many in our community to be one ounce of weight. However, the original measure of a *kazzayit* (meaning an olive) is basically a volume one, widely interpreted as 1/2 the volume of an average egg. (Although the olive was widely cited by the rabbis of old, it was supplanted by the egg for actual measurements.) The egg used for determining this measure must be an average one of the present time and locale. The weight measure we use today was derived from the volume; rabbis of the past calculated the volume and then weighed it for the convenience of the public.

A question has arisen with the one ounce of weight measure. An average to large size egg of today displaces approximately two fluid ounces. The cubic volume of one fluid ounce can be completely filled with less than 2/3 of an ounce (weight) of matzah. Thus, when eating the *mosi masah*, where it is preferable to eat two *kazzaytim*, one who is unable to eat two ounces may eat 1.33 ounces for two *kazzaytim*. Of course, as stated earlier, *bedi 'abad* one *kazzayit* is sufficient.

The measure for a *rebi 'it* wine is (just under) three fluid ounces. This is based on the Talmudic standard that a *rebi 'it* is the displacement of 1.5 eggs and on the fact that an average egg today displaces approximately two fluid ounces.

A *kazzayit* karpas or maror is of lesser weight than a *kazzayit* matzah as vegetables have a lower density of mass and thus a lower weight for the standard volume of half an egg's displacement.

X. Prayers

Each day of Pesah before arbit and during *shahrit*, we recite Psalm 107 which deals with various situations from which the psalmist was redeemed. The Pesah redemption is closely identified with all redemptions of the Almighty.

Ya 'ale veyabo is recited in each amida. If it was omitted during hol hamo'ed one repeats the amida. During yom tob it depends if mention of Pesah was made independently of it or not. *Ya 'ale veyabo* is also recited in Birkat Hamazon during Pesah.

After the amida of arbit the first two nights, complete Hallel is recited with berakhot.

Hallel is recited after the amida of *shahrit* each day. On the first two days the berakhot before and after are recited; on the latter days not. One explanation for the difference with Sukkot when we recite Hallel each day with berakhot is that the latter days of Pesah commemorate the drowning of the Egyptians at the Red Sea. The Midrash describes it as if the

Almighty said to the heavenly angels: "My creatures (the Egyptians) are drowning and you are singing?" So we tone down the Hallel recital by skipping parts (thus not saying the berakhot).

Specified Pesah selections are read from the Torah each morning. The minimum number of aliyot on yom tob is five plus maftir. The number of aliyot on hol hamo`ed is four. Even on hol hamo`ed two *Sifre Torah* are taken out each day.

Musaf prayer is recited daily.

We begin reciting *Morid Hatal* during Musaf of the first day and *Barekhenu* during the first weekday arbit of hol hamo`ed.

Tefillin are not donned during the days of Pesah.

Hallel on Israel Independence Day

The establishment of the State of Israel in 1948 was one of the most extraordinary events of modern times. Few events compare to it as regards inexplicability from a merely "natural" point of view. This is perhaps the unique instance of a People reclaiming its ancestral homeland after having largely been in exile from it for many centuries, in this case almost 1900 years.

Perhaps each particular in the amazing saga of modern Israel can be explained in a natural manner. But the larger picture is another story. Consider several of the numerous details:

In late 1947, the United Nations tried hard to persuade the Arabs to accept partition of Palestine into an Arab Palestinian state and a small Jewish state comprised of three non-contiguous land segments. It was widely understood that the Jewish state's viability would depend on the good will and cooperation of its neighbors. Despite the periodic Arab massacres of the previous generation, the Jews had accepted. But the Arabs refused. Hardly a single commentator on contemporary events is on record as having thought it possible that the next year would find a vibrant Jewish state founded on a contiguous territory much larger than had been proposed.

The armies of Egypt, Syria and Jordan, plus contingents from Iraq, Saudi Arabia and Lebanon invaded from all sides with military support from several other Arab nations. How the small Israeli army – that included many recently arrived survivors of the concentration camps – was able to vanquish the vastly superior numbers and arms of its enemies was astonishing.

Hallel on Israel Independence Day

As Israeli leaders – deeply committed to refrain from forced expulsion – were wondering how they could possibly cope with an Arab population larger than the Jewish one, Arab leaders made an astounding, inexplicable decision. They vigorously encouraged the Arab populace – on continuous radio broadcasts and in the press – to voluntarily depart (and return upon the supposed imminent victory). They even accused those who refused to leave of being traitors to the Arab cause. Thus, about 340,000 Arabs left Israel, greatly contributing to the viability of the new state. Reminiscing about this, President Moshe Sharett said, "A miracle happened and the Arabs fled."

Prompt international recognition was crucial for the new state. It was truly amazing that U.S. President Harry S. Truman extended recognition minutes after Israel declared independence. Remarkably, he ignored the strong recommendation of Secretary of State George C. Marshall as well as the State Department consensus not to do so. Indeed, when Washington called the U.S. Ambassador to the U.N. Warren Austin to notify him of the president's decision a few minutes before it was announced, his response was "that's impossible – we're making a pitch for trusteeship at this very moment." A member of the U.S. delegation was then addressing the General Assembly explaining why the U.S. preferred U.N. trusteeship rather than partition!

Can it be fully understood how the Arab nations, in a state of war with Israel, permitted 330,000 Jews living in their midst to emigrate to Israel during the first three years of the state? They may have had intentions of keeping Jewish property and crushing the fledgling state with masses of poor immigrants, but it turned out that they provided the new state with greatly increased strength and dynamism!

75

Hallel on Israel Independence Day

Before June 1967 it had widely been thought impossible for Israel to liberate East Jerusalem, Judea and Samaria in our times. The usually well-prepared Israel Defense Forces did not even have contingency battle plans for those areas. Experts considered it unfathomable that Jordan – who controlled those regions – even entered the war. It appears it was seduced by empty Egyptian boasts on the first day of that war of tremendous victories! Together with the conquest of the Sinai Peninsula and the Golan Heights, at the very least these Israeli victories created a previously unimagined opportunity for peace with its neighbors.

Who could have predicted the mighty ripple effects of the Six Day War, which pierced the "Iron Curtain," deeply stirring the Soviet Jewish community? In the first few years after that war over a quarter of a million Russian Jews were absorbed in Israel while an additional three-quarters of a million followed in succeeding years. Thus, a segment of world Jewry that had virtually been written off was redeemed while Israel was infused with vitally needed strength and skills.

However one views each detail, many of which may be interpreted as the result of great dedication, superior organizational ability, coincidence or good luck, surely the full constellation of events should be recognized by the traditional community as revealing the Almighty's Providence. From the apparently outrageous late 19th Century decision to make the dream of a reestablished homeland a reality in a mostly barren land devoid of adequate rainfall and natural resources, through steadfastness in the face of Arab opposition, Jewish controversy, world indifference, and the crushing blows of the Holocaust, to a blooming desert, internationally recognized statehood and military victories against enormous odds, dramatically revitalizing the Jewish People around the world, the full picture defies a "natural" interpretation. This meets the halakhic criteria of a miracle and requires a halakhic commemoration.

A traditional Jewish response to national miraculous events is to recite Hallel on the commemoration day (BT *Pesahim* 117a). Thus, we recite Hallel to commemorate the Exodus from Egypt and the events of Hanukah. We would also recite Hallel on Purim except – the Talmud informs us – that we have the Megillah to read or because the miracle occurred outside Israel or because we remained subjugated to Ahashverosh (BT *Megilla* 14a).

Given that the Land of Israel is the possession of the entire People; that oppressed Jews began emigrating to Israel; that Jews all over the world – many who had been on the verge of assimilation – began to identify with Israel; that Israel became the international center for Jewish studies and activities and a primary source of Jewish dignity; that Israel became the central focus of communal Jewish energy throughout the diaspora, the miracle was for all the Jewish People and it should be commemorated with Hallel.

Some rabbis make a distinction. Israel Independence Day, the fifth of Iyar, 1948, was not the day of deliverance from the war. The proclamation of independence escalated the war. Many lives were lost and as yet there has not truly been an end to the war. Additionally, sad to say, most members of the government and the populace are not observant of traditional Jewish Law. For these reasons, these authorities have stated that Israel Independence Day cannot be compared with the other days on which the Talmud states that Hallel is recited.

However, as the day that commemorates the Jewish People having reestablished their own government on their own land, to be concerned for the welfare of Jews all over the world and to work in the international arena for their protection; as the day the new Jewish government opened the doors to freedom for Jews everywhere, establishing a policy of granting automatic citizenship to every Jew who chooses to come and settle, thus ending the many centuries of Jewish homelessness and launching a massive Ingathering; as the day that brought most of the nations of the world to recognize a Jewish state and be more mindful of Jewish rights; and as the day that millions of Jews around the world felt revitalized and reattached themselves to the Jewish People, Independence Day is an event of great significance and happiness. It is an eminently appropriate occasion for special thanksgiving to the Almighty for His many present-day wonders and favors associated with Israel.

Thus, in the very first years of the state, the Council of the Chief Rabbinate of Israel, under the leadership of the chief rabbis of Israel, Rishon Lesion Rabbi Ben Sion Meir Hai Uziel and Rabbi Yishak Halevy Herzog, a"h, declared the appropriateness of reciting Hallel on Independence Day. However, acknowledging some distinctions from the classic cases of Hallel as explained above, it was decided to recite it without a berakha. This was also the position of our Brooklyn Sephardic community's chief rabbi, Rabbi Jacob S. Kassin, a"h.

It should be noted that in the succeeding years since 1948, as Israel was forced to war a number of times, and as on each occasion the Almighty rescued it from the danger of annihilation, the occasions for giving thanks have increased. As these wars occurred in a relatively short time span, and as each war's concluding events do not lend themselves to a clearly-defined specific commemorative day, Independence

Day has become the occasion for celebrating all of modern Israel's victories.

Some Sephardic rabbis, based on a statement of the great 18th Century decisor Rabbi Haim Yosef David Azulai (Rab Hida) have been reciting Hallel on Independence Day but not in its usual slot, immediately after the *amida* of *shahrit*. For kabbalistic reasons, Rab Hida states that when Hallel is recited for a miracle of lesser caliber than those of the Exodus or Hanukah, it should be said at prayer's end.

Regarding this point, the former Sephardic Chief Rabbi of Israel and Rishon Lesion Hakham Obadiah Yosef, *shlita*, wrote that if the congregation prefers to say Hallel on Israel Independence Day in the usual place they should not be stopped. Kabbalistic matters such as the one under discussion are only for those that understand them and keep them private (Yabia Omer v. 6, O.H. #41).

In our days, when many non-believers have denied the possibility of Divine intervention, and stubbornly insist on explaining the establishment of Israel in strictly natural terms, it would appear preferable to say Hallel in its usual place, not to give the impression that we are only reciting it as a compromise under pressure.

Regarding the day on which all Jerusalem was liberated and unified, Iyar 28, the Council of the Chief Rabbinate of Israel, under the leadership of then chief rabbis of Israel Rishon Lesion Rabbi Yishak Nessim and Rabbi Isar Yehuda Unterman, a"h, issued a proclamation to establish recital of Hallel with a *berakha* on Yom Yerushalayim. Although Iyar 28 was the third day of the Six Day War, the Chief Rabbinate considered the reunification of Jerusalem of historic significance in itself, and as it was part of and close to the conclusion of the miraculous victory that rescued the nation from the threat of annihilation, both commemorations were combined into one. Other rabbis, however, advocated Hallel without a *berakha* on this day also.

Of course halakhic Jews are grieved at the fact that modern Israel is far from being a halakhically observant country. Perhaps we can appreciate the position of those whose sensitivity to the widespread lack of traditional observance in modern Israel does not allow them to celebrate Independence Day in any way. Perhaps we may understand the position of those who even refuse to suspend the recital of *tahanunim* for the day. However, we cannot agree with them on these matters and should not pray with a minyan that recites *tahanunim* on this day. Not commemorating a national miracle in some appropriate manner is downgrading, even disgracing the miracle and an expression of ungratefulness to the Almighty. It strengthens the views of those who wish to say there has not been a miracle. Additionally, non-commemoration increases the disunity among the Jewish people and diminishes the possibility that the non-observant will be open to dialogue and receptive to the example and teachings of the observant.

The Almighty has provided us a great opportunity. We must do our part to make modern Israel succeed on the foundation of the Torah. This requires winning over the non-observant through education, friendliness, persuasion and good example. One of the most inspiring and efficacious approaches toward nurturing national unity and stirring religious feeling is undoubtedly through recognition of the miracle of modern Israel.

The late Sephardic Chief Rabbi of Israel Rishon Lesion Ben Sion Meir Hai Uziel captured the essence of the matter in a deathbed statement broadcast live on Israel radio in 1953:

Hallel on Israel Independence Day

Our generation has witnessed G-d's mighty and hidden hand as He gathered our dispersed to our ancestral land and brought us to dwell as a nation on its land... The Ingathering of recent decades was a seed... At the right moment He instilled counsel and courage in the hearts of our pioneers... and gave us the land.

Note this and reflect upon it greatly: these events are a result of G-d's fulfillment of his promise through his prophets for the good of Israel and the whole world. This good is contingent on Israel fulfilling Torah and mitzvot, thereby sanctifying the Name of the Holy One and bringing all nations to true faith in Him, resulting in universal peace...

Study Torah and teach it to your children, fulfill its statutes properly... Particularly preserve the peace of the People and the state. Controversy and divisiveness are our most dangerous enemies; peace and unity are the foundations of the survival of the Jewish state and the source of Divine blessing and strength for the Jewish People...

Rabbi Shamah's Response to Criticism on his "Recital of Hallel on Israel Independence Day" Article

Thank you for your response to my essay regarding Hallel on Israel Independence Day.

Regarding whether the post-Declaration of Independence Israeli leadership was deeply committed not to use transfer as a tactic – you are right that we should not be simplistic or naive. There usually are varied opinions among government leaders and undoubtedly there were some episodes of armed Jewish soldiers casting fear into the Arab populace.

However, despite some exceptions, it does appear to be the case that the Jewish leadership was committed not to use transfer.

Regarding whether Arab leaders called for evacuation in 1948, I think the widely held assumption that they did has not been refuted, but reinforced. Some Arabs departed at Jewish prompting but a tremendous number of them evacuated who could have remained had they chosen to. Anecdotal evidence often does not reflect the whole picture, but many who lived through the '48 events in Israel recall this situation. An elderly neighbor of ours, a man we have always found reliable, Mr. Dweck, who was living in Netanya in '48 and who had been living there since '34, insists that the local Jews pressed the local Arab residents to remain. The Jews were friendly with many Arabs and were not interested in being cruel to them. And they did not want to be seen that way. But, he clearly recalls, the Arabs were pressed by their leaders to evacuate.

Undoubtedly, some Arabs projected unto the Jews a disposition that they themselves might have had. Surely some feared that the Jews would take revenge for the 1920, 1929 and 1936 massacres. Scholars sometimes "reconstruct" what they believe must have been the case – to some degree it appears this was done with the so-called "massacre" at Deir Yassin – and in this case there may be other motivations also at work.

In any event, Moshe Sharett's use of the word "miracle" highlights the main point I referred to, namely, that an amazing, unpredictable, unexpected solution of evacuation came out of nowhere. The lack of coordination amongst Arab leaders that you cite as cause for much of the Arab disaster strengthens this perception.

Your points that prior to '48 the Yishuv was unfavorable to Jewish immigration from Arab countries and that until today discrimination against these Jews exists – disgraceful as these realities most certainly are – do not deny the point that the "population exchange" that took place immediately upon establishment of the state was an amazing phenomenon. It came out of nowhere and provided the state viability, despite the Ashkenazic prejudice.

It is true that historians [of the secular bent] do not see a miracle or Divine providence at work. But that is the case by definition – they reject the possibility before beginning their research. They would say the same for any miracle, so we cannot rely on them for evaluation.

Through the centuries, leading rabbinical figures often invoked the term "miracle" for events much less extraordinary than those under discussion. The huge, complex and unprecedented confluence of events leading to the establishment of Israel provided the Jewish world an opportunity for rejuvenation and deserves special recognition. Regarding the point of religion, it should be borne in mind that in Judaism's perspective, peoplehood, land and religion are interrelated.

My interpretation does follow that of several extraordinary spiritual leaders, including two rabbis whose greatness was universally recognized decades before establishment of the state and who both served as chief rabbis of Israel: Bension Hai Uziel and Isaac Halevy Herzog. A relevant portion from the former's 1953 statement on the subject was included in my essay; following is a 1956 statement from Rabbi Herzog that is included in the *Tikkun Yom Ha'Atzmaut*, Jerusalem, 1962:

It is my hope regarding this miracle which was for all the Jewish people, including our Diaspora brethren – which uplifted Israel's honor in the eyes of the nations; which infused new hope in the hearts of Israel after the terrible Holocaust; which strengthened the faith; and which provides our people a shelter until the coming of the Mashiah, in case that there will be persecutions of the nation anywhere – that all will agree that it is proper to set a commemoration day to strengthen our faith... I hope these [prayers] will penetrate the hearts of the Jewish people, including those *haredim* who stubbornly refuse to acknowledge this great miracle that G-d performed to us.

What the Jewish people have done with the opportunity presented them is another story. Had secularists had a slightly more "religious" response to events, had *haredi* elements chosen to be more receptive to the "miracle," and more forthcoming to the state and its populace, things would be very different. But we may be hopeful that the situation will change when and if peace finally comes.

By the way, population statistics do not bear you out that there was a [significant] indigenous Palestinian Arab people in Israel/Palestine prior to the Zionist movement. Careful studies of the half-century or so prior to 1948 have shown that as Jews came to settle and created economic opportunity, provided health care and raised living standards, Arabs from outside areas were attracted in great numbers. Most of the Arabs in what became Israel in 1948 – whose numbers have been wildly exaggerated – derived from other Arab lands, having arrived during the time of the increasing Jewish population. Antiquity of the Palestinian Arab communities for the most part is a modern myth created for political purposes. (See *From Time Immemorial* by Joan Peters, particularly chapters 11-12.)

On the Minhag of Studying Torah Leil Shabu`ot

Partly from the article written by Rabbi Asher Margaliot a"h for a Sephardic Institute publication.

The Magen Abraham, based on a Midrashic account, states: "At the Revelation at Sinai, when the time came for the Torah to be given, many fell asleep and the Almighty had to awaken them. We must rectify this through our staying awake and studying Torah through the night" (Orah Hayim 494). How many times during the year have we slept or idled away time during which we should have been studying Torah! How many times were we inattentive while listening to the Torah being read! Indeed, it is appropriate to express our regret at these shortcomings before commemorating receiving the Torah. The *Hoq Ya'aqob*, based on the Zohar, explains that the pious remain awake and labor in Torah all night as an expression of eagerness and anticipation for a great, precious event. "Let us go to our possession, the sacred inheritance designated for us and our children". The Zohar commends those who thus could anticipate the hour of receiving the Torah, when the people of Israel became joined to the Torah and both became as one. Rabbi Israel Nagara elaborates thus: "since the hour of the giving of the Torah is, as it were, the hour of wedding between Israel and the Torah, it is proper to be engaged in preparing the ornaments of the bride the previous night".

The Rambam, in codifying our ancient traditions regarding the approach to the study of Torah all year long, states: "A person learns most of his wisdom by night." Perhaps the later rabbis chose to establish the main learning of Shabu`ot at night to also reflect this concept.

85

The *Shelah Haqadosh* relates that on *Leil Shabu`ot* the Divine Presence was revealed to Maran Rabbi Yosef Karo and his companions, who were studying Torah all that night, and said to them: "Happy are you and happy is your portion." Those who dedicate their speech, actions and thought to Torah study on this night more readily merit the revelation of the Torah's intricacies and achieve a deeper understanding in their learning.

The Kabbalah sages prescribed an order of study, or *tiqqun*, for *Leil Shabu`ot*, comprising passages from each parasha and each Book of the written Torah, plus selections from Mishnah and Zohar. The Ten Commandments are read twice. Megillat Ruth is entirely read as it relates the inspiring story of a non-Jewess fully turning to Judaism.

Some communities read a brief synopsis of the 613 mitzvot. Some communities, in accordance with the Midrashic statement that the Torah was very difficult to understand until Mishle was written, read the entire Book of Mishle, for its parables contain the key to much of the Torah.

Regarding those not initiated into the Kabbalah, reading the Zohar portions of the *tiqqun*, or any other portions of Zohar, there are two opinions. Some say reading Zohar is "good for the soul" even if one does not understand what he is reading. Others claim that it is more appropriate to skip the Zohar and study those portions of the Torah which one may understand.

The *Hoq Ya'aqob* is of the opinion that the *tiqqun* was established for the unlearned, but a scholar may study whatever Torah subject his heart desires. In many great Ashkenazic yeshivot the custom of staying up all night was observed but the order of study was Talmud, not the *tiqqun*.

Today many scholars do follow the practice of reading the *tiqqun* on this night.

The *Ben Ish Hai* writes that even if one cannot stay up all night for whatever reason, he should nonetheless recite the Tanakh portion of the *tiqqun*.

May we all continue to go from strength to strength and merit rewards for our study and contemplation of Torah especially on this Festival of the Giving of the Torah.

Halakhot of Ta`anit Sibbur
(Public Fast Days)

I. Overview

There are six fast days in the Jewish calendar. One, Yom Kippur, is from the Torah. Four of the five others are from the days of the Prophets specifically referred to by Hashem in a communication to the Prophet Zechariah: "The fast of the fourth month, the fast of the fifth month, the fast of the seventh month, and the fast of the tenth month shall become occasions for joy and gladness, happy festivals for the House of Judah; but you must love emet and shalom" (Zech. 8:19).

These four are associated with the vanquishing of Jerusalem, destruction of the Bet Hamiqdash and the extinguishing of the last flame of the first Jewish Commonwealth in 586 B.C.E. and the corresponding events destroying the Second Temple in 70 C.E. The sixth fast day is associated with Purim.

Following are the names, dates and events commemorated (in calendrical order):

1. *Shib'a Asar B'Tammuz*, the 17th day of Tamuz (the fourth month from Nissan, the month of the Exodus, declared to be the first of the months). This is the date the Romans broke through Jerusalem's walls in 70 C.E. In 586 B.C.E. the Babylonians broke through Jerusalem's walls on the 9th of Tamuz, but the fast date was modified to reflect the later destruction, as it is that destruction that still prevails. The Talmud relates that on this day in different years four other national calamities befell the Jewish People: the Tablets were broken; the daily *tamid* sacrifice was terminated in the First Temple; the Roman Emperor

Vespasian burned the Sefer Torah and placed an idol in the Temple.

2. Tisha B'ab - 9th of Ab (the fifth month, the fast being exactly three weeks after the 17th of Tammuz). The Mishnah relates that on this date the destruction of both the first and second Temples occurred and three other national calamities befell the Jewish People: Hashem's decree denying entry to the Land of Israel to the generation that exited Egypt, because of the transgression associated with the spies, that the people were fearful of proceeding to the land, capture of the great city of Bethar (by the Romans in 135 C. E., crushing the Bar Kokhba revolution) and the ploughing of Jerusalem (see Jer. 26:18).

3. Saum Gedalya, on the 3rd of Tishri, the seventh month. Gedalya ben Ahiqam, who had been appointed by the victorious Babylonians as the Jewish governor of Judea after the sacking of Jerusalem, officially permitting a remnant of the nation to remain in the land, was assassinated in an act of political treason and the remnant went to Egypt. This ended over six hundred consecutive years of Israelite government in the Land of Israel, which was not restored for seventy years. The event occurred on the first of Tishri 586 B.C.E., but out of consideration for Rosh Hashanah it is commemorated on the day following the holiday.

4. Asara Betebet - 10th of Tebet, the tenth month. The day the long and devastating siege of Jerusalem began in 588 B.C.E.

5. Ta`anit Esther - 13th of Adar, the day before Purim. Placed approximately 527 B.C.E. It commemorates the fasting and repentance the people engaged in the day before the scheduled battle with Haman's followers.

Halakhot of Ta`anit Sibbur (Public Fast Days)

Yom Kippur and Tisha B'ab are the only 24 hour (plus) fast days, beginning at sunset and concluding the next evening (at 'the appearance of the stars'). The other four begin at dawn (1.2 proportionate hours before sunrise) and conclude at evening. Yom Kippur and Tisha B'ab also each have a number of unique halakhot. Halakhot of Yom Kippur and of Tisha B'ab will be discussed in their separate sections. The following will deal with the other four fast days only.

II. General Halakhot of Fast Days (Excluding Yom Kippur and Tisha B'ab)

All eating and drinking, even of a small measure, is prohibited. Sick and very weak people whose health requires eating or drinking are exempt. (Of course this refers to a sickness that does not pose a threat to life; in cases of life-threatening sicknesses one must eat even on Yom Kippur.) Someone close to becoming sick, who by fasting might become sick, is also exempt. Someone who is able to fast but must take medicine may do so providing it is not pleasant tasting and he does not take water (or any drink) with it.

Pregnant women are exempt as are those who gave birth within twenty four months before the fast.

Children are discouraged from fasting these fasts before becoming obligated in mitzvot (twelve years of age for girls, thirteen for boys).

If one mistakenly ate, regardless of how much, he should continue the fast from the moment he remembered. If he ate less than a *kazzayit* he is still considered fasting and should recite anenu in the amida.

If by mistake one recited the berakha on a food item, he should eat a tiny amount not to let the berakha be in vain.

Taking showers and wearing fresh clothing are permitted. Brushing teeth and gargling mouthwash are permitted provided one does not swallow.

When one of these fasts falls on a Shabbat the fast is pushed forward to Sunday. In the case of Ta`anit Esther, as the Sunday would be Purim, it is pushed back to Thursday.

Abi Haben (the father who had *mila* performed to his son that day), the *sandaq* (the one who held the boy) and the *mohel* (the one who performed the circumcision), although they participated in a great and joyous mitzvah, are not exempt from fasting except on Ta`anit Esther. However, when the *b'rit* is on one of these fast days that was pushed off from Shabbat, they are permitted to eat after mid-day. The same applies to a bride and groom within the seven days after their wedding.

III. Prayers

In the amida a special prayer *anenu* is recited by all who are fasting in the midst of the berakha *Shema Qolenu*. The individual does not recite a berakha for *anenu*, whether praying alone or with a minyan. If he forgot to recite it he does not repeat the amida. If he remembered before concluding the amida, he should recite it at the end, before saying *Oseh Shalom*.

In hazara, the hazzan recites anenu with a concluding berakha between the seventh and eighth berakhot (between *Go'el* and *Rophe*).

Halakhot of Ta`anit Sibbur (Public Fast Days)

The hazzan should be one who is fasting except in the circumstance when none of those fasting can competently so serve. In the latter case the hazzan may recite anenu although not personally fasting, as his prayer is on behalf of the public.

If a hazzan forgot to say anenu in hazara and remembers or is reminded after he concluded the eighth berakha (*Refa'enu*) but before concluding *Shema Qolenu*, he should say it in the midst of *Shema Qolenu* as the individual does, without the additional berakha. If he forgot it even there, he does not return and does not repeat the amida.

In a minyan praying *Beqol Ram*, that is when the hazzan prays silently after the first three berakhot, he should recite the anenu berakha aloud in its usual place in hazara with its berakha. The other members of the minyan, at whatever spot of their amida they are in, should be attentive, listening silently and not answer amen in the middle of their amida. They should recite anenu in the usual place it is recited in the silent amida, in *Shema Qolenu*. The hazzan should not recite it again.

A special selection is read from the Torah both in *shahrit* and minha from *Perashat Ki Tissa* recounting Moshe Rabenu's prayer after Israel's transgression of the golden calf and Hashem's favorable response to Moshe's prayer. Only those fasting should receive aliyot.

For the hazzan to recite anenu as a separate berakha in hazara, and for the minyan to read the special portion from the Torah, it is proper there should be ten fasting. Nevertheless, if only six members of the minyan are fasting both the above are permitted.

If there are not at least six members of the minyan fasting, the hazzan does not recite anenu between *Go'el* and *Rophe* but in *Shema Qolenu* as the individual does, without a berakha. If it is Monday or Thursday morning, the regular portion for that week is read from the Torah; in minha, and on Sunday, Tuesday, Wednesday or Friday mornings, the Torah is not read.

Many have a custom to don tefillin for minha. The purpose is either to have an opportunity to recite additional berakhot to arrive at the recommended daily minimum of one hundred or to provide additional sanctity on the fast day. In early 20th Century Aleppo this custom was not universal and most other Sephardic communities do not have it. It is optional. Thus, if one finds it difficult to get his tefillin for minha, he may pray without them. If one finds himself in a minha minyan where the congregation is not donning tefillin he should not feel required to don them and he may be given an aliya and be hazzan.

Birkat Kohanim is recited in minha only when minha is prayed close to sunset (the time *ne'ila* would be said on Yom Kippur). A kohen who is not fasting does not recite *Birkat Kohanim* in minha.

Halakhot of Tisha B'ab

I. Overview

The fast of the Ninth of Ab, referred to by the prophet Zechariah, was established as a national mourning day commemorating destruction of the Bet Hamiqdash, sacked on that day by the Babylonians in 586 B.C.E. The Mishnah (Ta`anit 4:6) relates that four other national calamities occurred in various years on this day: the Almighty's decree that the 'Generation of the Wilderness' be denied entry to the Land of Israel because of the transgression associated with the spies; destruction of the Second Temple (by the Romans in 70 C.E.); capture of the great city Bethar (the last stronghold of Bar Kokhba in the revolution he led, 7 miles southwest of Jerusalem, by the Romans in 135 C.E.); and Jerusalem was ploughed like a field (see Jer. 26:18).

The full degree of mourning is limited to Tisha B'ab day itself. Secondary rituals beginning prior to the fast day were established in the course of time, which are increased in intensity as the day approaches.

The ultimate purpose of the fast days is to foster repentance and increase the national commitment to Torah and mitzvot. The giving of charity to the needy is essential on these days.

II. The Three Weeks

The three weeks beginning with the 17th of Tammuz through the 9th of Ab have often been times of adversity for the Jewish People. However, the sages did not establish formal restrictions until Rosh Hodesh Ab, as they did not wish to add to the nation's burden. We have been advised to be more cautious than usual with potentially dangerous situations during these days of dejection.

Halakhot of Tisha B'ab

It is a Sephardic custom to refrain from eating 'new' fruit during the three weeks so as to avoid reciting *sheheheyanu*. This berakha is a joyful thanksgiving expression and it is difficult to mention *lazeman hazeh* with the requisite happy heart during these days. We also desist from wearing new clothing during the three weeks. However, at a b'rit milah *sheheheyanu* is recited. On Shabbat, it is permitted to partake of 'new' fruit and recite *sheheheyanu* and wear new clothing.

Some Sephardic communities, as do virtually all Ashkenazic communities, desist from having weddings and musical functions for the three weeks. Most Sephardic communities, as is the practice in Israel, following Shulhan Arukh, desist for nine days only, beginning Rosh Hodesh Ab. For many decades the Aleppo-derived Brooklyn Syrian community has not held weddings during the three weeks.

III. The Nine Days

Beginning Rosh Hodesh Ab we refrain from optional festive occasions and reduce joyful pursuits. This includes purchases of luxuries, new clothing and wedding accoutrements. If a wedding is shortly after Tisha B'ab and time is of the essence, necessary shopping is permitted. We refrain from home decorating during these days.

We refrain from meat, including chicken, and wine during these days. Out of respect for Rosh Hodesh, the Syrian community begins these latter stringencies from the second of the month.

Meat and wine are permitted on Shabbat during the nine days as well as at a *se'udat misvah*, such as a b'rit milah or *siyyum masekhta* (concluding study of a Talmudic tractate). Habdalah wine is permitted.

95

One may have meat during these days if required for health purposes such as may be the case with an anemic person, a nursing or pregnant woman or one who gave birth within thirty days.

The Syrian community's custom has been to eat meat leftovers from Shabbat during the nine days providing that one did not purposely cook extra for this purpose. Most other Sephardic communities are strict on this. Many authorities hold that with the advent of efficient freezers it is now proper to be strict.

IV. The Week During Which Tisha B'ab Occurs

After the Shabbat that precedes Tisha B'ab through Tisha B'ab itself is the 'Week of Tisha B'ab.' If Tisha B'ab falls on a Sunday or on Shabbat - in which case the fast is pushed to Sunday - there is no 'Week of.'

During the 'Week of,' the following are prohibited:
a) Washing the whole body with hot or warm water. Showering or bathing in cold water is permitted. A little warm water may be mixed in to break the chill.
b) Wearing fresh clothes. It is advisable to accumulate slightly worn garments from before the 'Week of' to change into. Something worn a half-hour is no longer 'fresh.'
c) Washing clothing even to wear after Tisha B'ab. Washing garments of little children, who constantly soil them, is permitted.
d) Haircuts and shaving. A man who normally shaves daily or every other day, and is required to shave for business reasons, may do so except on Tisha B'ab day itself.

V. Se`udat Hamafseqet

The last meal before the fast, when taking place on a weekday, should be plain, comprised of bread and water with, at most, one cooked dish. If the dish preparation normally comprises more than one item, such as eggs and tomatoes, it is acceptable. Fish is too luxurious for this meal. Uncooked vegetables and tea or coffee are permitted to be added to this meal.

For this meal, it is customary to choose an item that symbolizes mourning, such as a hard-boiled egg or lentils.

One sits alone on the floor for this meal. Even if three men are in the same room they do not recite zimmun before birkat hamazon.

When the last meal occurs on Shabbat there are no restrictions; one may eat meat, drink wine and enjoy a most festive meal together with family or friends.

VI. Tisha B'ab Night and Day

Tisha B'ab prohibitions apply from the sunset beginning the day until "appearance of the stars" the following evening, in the New York area about 30 minutes after sunset. The following are prohibited: eating, drinking, washing the body, anointing, wearing leather shoes and marital relations.

Studying Torah, which gladdens the heart, is also prohibited, except for the study of sad subjects. The obligation to study Torah daily, however, applies to Tisha B'ab. It is customary to study Lamentations (Ekha), the Book of Job, the sad portions in Jeremiah and the Talmudic account of the destruction. The commentaries on these texts are also permitted to be read.

One who is sick, even if the sickness does not pose danger to life, is exempt. One who senses he/she is becoming sick or would become sick upon continuing the fast may break it. Pregnant and nursing women, although straightaway exempt from the other rabbinical fasts, if healthy, are required to fast on Tisha B'ab, unless they are extremely weak. A woman who gave birth within thirty days before Tisha B'ab is exempt. When Tisha B'ab falls on Shabbat and the fast is pushed to Sunday, which lessens its status, pregnant and nursing women are exempt.

When Tisha B'ab falls on Sunday or on Shabbat and the fast is pushed to Sunday, one who is permitted to eat must first make habdala. In such a case it is proper to have a minor listen to the berakha on the wine or grape juice and drink from it since we should not drink wine on this day. If a minor is not available the person making habdala may drink from the wine him/herself.

Washing of hands, including *netilat yadayim*, is up to the knuckles. Washing other parts of the body, whether in hot or cold water, is forbidden. One uses the dampness of the towel to wipe away the sediment from the eyes in the morning. Even after using the bathroom, or when one has touched a covered part of the body, washing is up to the knuckles. However, if somehow a part of the body became dirty or very sweaty, it is permitted to wash in a limited way, for the essential prohibition of washing is when done for pleasure.

Application of medication or deodorant is permitted. Those for whom brushing teeth is as a necessity, that they are extremely bothered when they do not brush, may do so in a minimal manner.

Non-leather sneakers with non-structural leather ornamentation are permitted. Leather garments other than shoes are permitted.

It is customary to sit on the floor as a mourner at night and in the day until minha. Laughter and levity are prohibited all day. If greetings are extended, one may respond but in a subdued manner.

In past centuries many communities established a custom not to work on Tisha B'ab. However, even in those communities it was permitted to work to prevent depreciation of capital or to take advantage of an unusual passing opportunity. The manner in which the modern economic system is structured, most businesses involve significant loss of capital when one closes as there are numerous fixed expenses, including payroll, rent and utilities. Thus, in our days most businesses are permitted to be open and most people are permitted to work. The rabbis said that those that can be off from work without causing significant loss should do so to more fully participate in the mourning.

When there is a milah on Tisha B'ab, the father, *sandaq* and *mohel* are not permitted to break their fast. However, when Tisha B'ab falls on Shabbat and the fast is pushed to Sunday, these three are permitted to curtail their fast and eat after an early minha.

All that is prohibited on Tisha B'ab is permitted immediately at the conclusion of the day except for eating meat and drinking wine. As a remembrance to the fire that continued burning in the Bet Hamiqdash through the next day, we refrain from these until the conclusion of the following day. When Tisha B'ab falls on Shabbat and is pushed to Sunday, we only refrain from eating meat and drinking wine during the night immediately following the fast.

When the fast begins on Saturday night, the habdalah on wine at the conclusion of Shabbat is recited Sunday night. *Boreh Me'oreh Ha'esh*, the blessing commemorating the creation of fire, however, is recited Saturday night.

VII. Prayers

On the afternoon preceding the fast most congregations pray minha early to allow partaking of a regular meal such that there would be a respectable interval between it and *se'udat mafseqet*, which is eaten close to sunset.

Tahanun supplications (ana) are not recited in minha before Tisha B'ab or on Tisha B'ab day, as it is called *mo'ed* in *Megillat Ekha*. Although in peshat this usage refers to a date for destruction, the midrash expounds it as indicating that eventually it will become a positive occasion and thus a great prompt for hope and redemption.

To create a suitable atmosphere, synagogue lights are dimmed during evening and morning services.

In most Aleppo-derived communities, Ha'azinu is recited before arbit and in *shahrit* in place of Az Yashir. It is generally chanted in unison by the congregation.

Ekha and various qinot (elegies) are recited both in the evening and morning services. In most Aleppo-derived communities Ekha is read before arbit; as Rabbi Matloub Abady a"h wrote, citing the 1525 *Mahzor Aram Soba*, this was a pre-Shulhan Arukh Aleppo custom. In virtually all other communities, following Shulhan Arukh, Ekha is read after arbit.

Anenu is recited in all three amidot of the day. *Nahem* is recited in the *Boneh Yerushalayim* berakha of the amida. Following Shulhan Arukh, many Sephardic communities

100

recite *Nahem* in all three amidot. Aleppo-derived communities recite it only in minha. The amida is not repeated if one forgot to recite *Anenu* or *Nahem*. Since the establishment of the modern state of Israel, particularly since 1967, many recite a modified version of *Nahem* so that it should be in harmony with the reality of today. They deem it problematic to stand in prayer before the Almighty and say of Jerusalem, "she dwells without her children," etc.

Qaddish Titqabal is not recited in arbit. It is recited in the other prayers.

The Sefer Torah is read in *shahrit* and minha. There is a haftara reading in *shahrit*. Most Sephardic communities also read a haftara in minha. The Aleppo community, however, does not, based on *HaRambam*.

Following Shulhan Arukh, *shahrit* should not be prayed with talet and tefillin, emphasizing the mourning nature of the day. Talet and tefillin are donned for minha. Some don tefillin privately at home in the morning, recite shema, remove them, and come to synagogue for prayers. Some members of Aleppo-derived communities even pray individually at home until after the amida and come to synagogue for Sefer Torah, Ekha and qinot. In our days, when people from different communities and different customs congregate for prayers, it is most advisable to follow Shulhan Arukh and pray with a minyan in synagogue without talet and tefillin.

At the conclusion of minha selected comforting verses from Tanakh are recited.

תזכו בנחמת ציון

Selihot

by Rabbi Ronald Barry Rabbi, Sephardic Institute

The custom of waking up early in the pre-morning hours to recite Selihot during the 40 days from Rosh Hodesh Elul until Yom Kippur is codified in Shulhan Arukh (Orah Hayim 581:1). The Selihot prayers were designed to facilitate Teshubah (repentance) in preparation for the annual Day of Judgement.

In recent years people have asked: should all men attend Selihot daily or are people in certain occupations or situations exempt from attending on a regular basis? One specific question addressed by Rabbi Obadia Yosef (Yehave Da`at 3:44, Yabi`a Omer 2: A.H. 28, Yalqut Yosef Mo`adim: Hilkhot Selihot) is regarding yeshiva students, kolel men, and Rabbis, who normally study Torah late into the night and whose studies would be affected negatively by attending early Selihot daily. He applies the same question to workers and teachers who, as a result of attending early Selihot daily, would not be giving their employers their full and appropriate efforts and attention. Are these groups exempt from daily Selihot? If they do attend daily and their studies or work are affected negatively, should they stop attending?

The approach taken by Rabbi Obadia Yosef is first to see how extensive the custom of daily Selihot from Rosh Hodesh Elul was historically. (He does not mention it but it is generally known that among Ashkenazim Selihot is nonexistent until a few days before Rosh Hashanah, although they do blow shofar from Rosh Hodesh Elul).

However, among the Eastern and Sephardic communities he quotes numerous Geonim and Rishonim (many already

Selihot

cited in the *Tur* - Orah Hayim 581:1) who attest to several different customs regarding what days to say Selihot. These customs include:

1. Only the days between Rosh Hashanah and Yom Kippur, Asseret Yeme Teshubah (Rab Hai Gaon, Rab Amram, Rab Cohen Sedek, Rambam, Rab Abraham Bar Natan Hayarhi, custom in the Gerona, Spain area);
2. From the 25th of Elul (custom in the Barcelona, Spain area)
3. Mondays and Thursdays in Elul in addition to Asseret Yeme Teshubah (Me'iri)
4. 40 days from Rosh Hodesh Elul to Yom Kippur (Certain portions of Spain).

Once established that other customs were prevalent or perhaps dominant historically in Sephardic communities, even though Shulhan Arukh codifies the 40-day custom, Rabbi Obadia Yosef maintains that people in the above-mentioned occupations can or should rely on these other customs of trying to attend only on Mondays and Thursdays in Elul and during Asseret Yeme Teshubah. He also disagrees with the approach of the Hida in *Birke Yosef* who says that during this time of year it is better to increase our reciting communal Selihot and lessen personal Torah study.

Rabbi Obadia Yosef brings no precedent or source supporting his partial exemption for *Talmide Hakhamim*, teachers and workers who are faced with the conflict of fulfilling other obligations as opposed to fulfilling the current Selihot custom.

Other related questions on this issue:

103

Selihot

1. Would these *Talmide Hakhamim* and workers be exempt even if the 40-day custom was the only one historically? Should logic and ethics not also apply here?
2. What about the desired result of Teshubah that Selihot may cause? Would that outweigh all other considerations?
3. What about negative effects of early waking on other aspects of life and relationships - such as family life and responsibilities or other mitzvot like Bikur Holim, or communal obligations?
4. How does the possibility of reciting Selihot during daylight such as before Minha affect this issue?

Is the approach of taking into account non-Shulhan Arukh customs legitimate? Would it also apply to laws as well as to customs?

Halakhot of Rosh Hashanah

I. Selihot

Beginning the day after Rosh Hodesh Elul (the month before Rosh Hashanah), and concluding the day before Yom Kippur, selihot are recited early each weekday morning before *shahrit*. These are special prayers designed to facilitate teshubah (repentance). It is inappropriate to arrive at the annual Day of Judgment, as the first day of the new year is called, without having prepared beforehand.

II. General Laws and Customs

Since Rosh Hashanah is the beginning of the year (and commemorates G-d's creation of the world), it also is the Day of Judgment of humans. One's thoughts should focus on the Creator, acknowledging His kingship and His desire that we strive to improve ourselves spiritually and endeavor to make the world a better place for all in accordance with His will. We must be serious about these matters and not engage in lightheaded behavior. It is necessary to dress modestly.

Although it is the Day of Judgment, we are to express our confidence that the Almighty will accept our prayers and repentance and inscribe us for a year of life. Thus, it is prohibited to fast on Rosh Hashanah and the mitzvah of *simhat yom tob* (happiness of the holiday) applies just as on the three festivals; there should be a festive meal both at night and in the day.

During the evening meal, after *qiddush* and *hamosi*, we eat special foods with an appropriate prayer for each that through their names or nature prompt optimistic thoughts for the new year. Some communities have this custom only the first night, some both nights. It is customary to dip the *hamosi* in sugar (some use honey) instead of salt and not eat "sour" dishes throughout Rosh Hashanah.

The berakha of *sheheheyanu* is recited in *qiddush* both nights just as on both first nights of all yamim tobim. However, Shulhan Arukh states it is preferable to have a "new" fruit on the table the second night and direct the *sheheheyanu* toward it also. The reason is that there is a group of *posqim* who consider the two days of Rosh Hashanah as one long day halakhically and according to them *sheheheyanu* should not be recited the second night for the day itself. Having a new fruit removes any doubt concerning the *sheheheyanu*. (Reciting an unnecessary berakha is a violation of our responsibility to respect G-d's name.) In this particular case, however, in the final analysis, if one did not have a new fruit or another new item toward which the *sheheheyanu* could be directed, it is recited anyway, for it is not a true doubt.

In some respects, the two days of Rosh Hashanah are considered as a single halakhic day. Thus, the halakha that permits the use of medicines when there is no danger to life on the second day of yamim tobim does not apply to the second day of Rosh Hashanah. Even in Israel, Rosh Hashanah is celebrated two days, unlike other yamim tobim.

It is preferable not to sleep during the day of Rosh Hashanah, but rather to study Torah. If one finds himself in a situation where he cannot concentrate on studying Torah and is idling away his time in gossip, etc., it is preferable to sleep.

III. Prayers

It is traditional to sing the poetic works of great rabbis on the exalted themes of Rosh Hashanah and Yom Kippur with melodies special for the occasion. Rosh Hashanah is ushered in with the singing of *Ahot Qetana*.

The amida of Rosh Hashanah and Yom Kippur emphasizes the kingship of the Almighty and includes additions reflecting the vision of a world in harmony and peace fulfilling His will.

It is customary to have assistants to the right and left of the hazzan during the prayers of these special days.

Additions to Prayers: Hashem Hu Ha'elokim is recited before Hashem Melekh, Shir Hama`alot Mima`amakim after Yishtabah, Abinu Malkenu after the amida of *shahrit* and minha. Hamelekh Haqadosh is said in place of Hakel Haqadosh in the amida. Several additional insertions are made in the amida as found in all mahzorim.

Torah and Haftarah Readings: On the first day the Torah reading begins with Hashem's 'remembering' Sarah (with childbirth). A portion about Rosh Hashanah is read from a second Sefer Torah. The haftarah is about Hashem's 'remembering' Hannah. The second day Torah reading is about G-d's test of Abraham with Aqedat Yishaq. The portion read from the second Sefer Torah is the same as the first day. The haftarah, from the prophet Jeremiah, is about Hashem's remembering, and love for, Israel.

Musaf: The musaf prayer of Rosh Hashanah includes three special sections reflecting the essence of the day. Each section comprises ten verses from Tanakh and concludes with a berakha. The first section focuses on G-d's kingship

מלכויות; the second on His remembrances for judgment זכרונות; the third on the significance of the shofar שופרות.

Tashlikh: In the afternoon of the first day the custom is to recite '*Tashlikh*', a symbolic 'casting away of sins'. It is preferable to recite it by the banks of a body of water but if a natural body of water is not available, it is acceptable to fill a pool. One who did not recite this prayer on Rosh Hashanah should do so during Asseret Yeme Teshubah.

IV. Shofar

It is a Torah commandment to hear the shofar blasts on the day of Rosh Hashanah. The shofar is associated with the coronation of a king and helps us focus on the importance of recognizing and accepting Hashem as our king. In addition, in the Books of the Prophets the shofar is associated with the signal of the city watchman who warns that the enemy is arriving. On the Day of Judgment the Shofar is the alarm that we are faced with an emergency; it awakens us from our slumber and calls us to repent. The shofar also recalls the ram substituted for the sacrifice of Yishaq. It is also associated with the Giving of the Torah and the Ingathering of the Exiles.

Women are not obligated to hear the shofar as it is a positive mitzvah governed by time. Nevertheless, they fulfill a mitzvah if they hear it.

Children who have reached the age of understanding should be brought to synagogue to hear the shofar but only if they do not disturb others.

The *toke'ah* (shofar blower) should stand. For the first series of blasts the congregation remains seated.

The *toke`ah* must have intentions that his blowing is for the mitzvah and that others may fulfill their obligation through hearing his blowing. The listener must also have intent to fulfill his obligation.

Two berakhot are recited before blowing the shofar the first time: *Lishmo`ah Qol Shofar* and *Sheheheyanu*. One who has fulfilled his obligation of shofar earlier in the day and is blowing only for others may still recite the berakhot.

The complete mitzvah comprises one hundred individual blasts. They are blown in eight series. The first series, before musaf, comprises thirty blasts. The other seven series comprise ten blasts each: three series in the quiet amida, three in the hazara and one in the *qaddish* after the amida. It is customary to blow a 101st blast, a *teru`ah gedola*, before Alenu.

When Rosh Hashanah occurs on Shabbat the shofar is not blown and it is *muqseh*. Although from Torah law the shofar should be blown even on Shabbat, the rabbis prohibited it, fearing it might lead to carrying on Shabbat.

V. Asseret Yeme Teshubah

The ten days from Rosh Hashanah through Yom Kippur are singularly designated and dedicated to Teshubah. Although Teshubah is accepted any time, it is accepted even more readily during these days.

For the above reason it has been traditional that Jewish people give more charity and do more good deeds during these days. It is the time when they express their religious identity.

Shulhan Arukh states that it is proper for those accustomed to eating bread baked by non-Jews all year long (known to be kosher, an item that is permitted to eat) to refrain from doing so these days. It is an example of a stringency accepted for these days.

Prayers: During Asseret Yeme Teshubah a person should pray more carefully than usual. Six insertions and substitutions are made in the amida as found in all siddurim.

VI. Teshubah - Repentance

Aspects of complete Teshubah:

1. Viduy - recognition of the sin and confession to Hashem. When done silently it is proper to specify the particular transgression.
2. Abandoning the sinful practice
3. Feeling of regret for having done the sin
4. Resolution for the future

In making a resolution for the future, it is proper, often necessary, to devise a strategy to cope with temptation. It is appropriate to build a 'fence' around the transgression, that will prevent one from crossing the line, each person as fits his/her situation.

Just as one must repent of sins involving actions, so must one repent of any evil dispositions that he may have, such as an angry temper, hatred, jealousy, greedy pursuit of money and honor, gluttony, etc.

Sins against one's fellow man are not forgiven by the Almighty until the sinner has received forgiveness from the injured party and repents.

Hatarat Nedarim (Annulment of Vows): As the sin of broken vows is very serious, it is customary to make Hatarat Nedarim before Rosh Hashanah, to clean the slate as much as possible. We also declare our intention not to vow in the future. Hatarat Nedarim is not a prayer but a declaration to the Bet Din requesting annulment of the vow, which is possible if the individual requesting is deeply regretful for having made the vow. If one did not make a vow Hatarat Nedarim is inapplicable.

Hamelekh HaMishpat During Asseret Yeme Teshubah

Along the lines of Hakham Obadia Yosef's pesaq

The Gemara (B. Berakhot 12) states that during Asseret Yeme Teshubah we conclude the Ata Qadosh blessing with *Hamelekh Haqadosh* and the *Hashiba* blessing with *Hamelekh Hamishpat*, and one who does not recite the required formula does not fulfill his obligation. The Gemara speaks about both in the same sentence, indicating one halakha for both. Commentators disagree on the implication of "does not fulfill his obligation". The majority of classical commentators (Rishonim) interpret it as it was eventually codified by Rabbi Joseph Karo in Shulhan Arukh OH 582:1 (1564):

If one realized he did not mention Hamelekh Haqadosh or *Hamelekh Hamishpat* after concluding the amida he repeats the amida; if he realized in mid-amida he returns. Regarding *Hamelekh Haqadosh* he returns to the beginning of the amida [as the first three berakhot are one unit]; in the case of *Hamelekh Hamishpat* he returns to the beginning of *Hashiba*.

A minority view of classical commentators state that the Gemara's "does not fulfill his obligation" in this case does not mean repeat or return, but that the mitzvah was not performed appropriately. Both Shulhan Arukh and the Ramah, Rabbi Joseph Karo's younger contemporary who usually represents Ashkenazic practice in his glosses on Shulhan Arukh, ignored this minority view.

A third view, that of a single classical commentator, agrees with the first view as regards the meaning of "does not

Asseret Yeme Teshubah

fulfill his obligation" (repeat/return), but maintains that in our days it does not apply to *Hamelekh Hamishpat*. He is of the opinion that in Talmudic days the all-year-long concluding phrase of *Hashiba* did not include the word *Melekh*; since somehow the text of the berakha was changed to include *Melekh* (*Melekh Oheb Sedaka Umishpat*), if one made a mistake during Asseret Yeme Teshubah and concluded as he does all year long, he would have mentioned the key words and fulfilled his obligation. According to this opinion it is not critical to say exactly Hamelekh Hamishpat. Ramah cited this view in his glosses on Shulhan Arukh (1569) and it has been the accepted Ashkenazic practice.

Many have wondered how it came about that the Ashkenazic practice followed one classic commentary who interprets the Gemara differently from the overwhelming majority of classical commentators.

Furthermore, the phrase established for Asseret Yeme Teshubah, *Hamelekh Hamishpat*, brings to an individual's consciousness one of the underlying motifs of these special days - the Almighty ascending His Throne of Justice to decide the fate of each individual. This thought is not expressed in the all-year-long phrase of "The King Who loves righteousness and justice". In contemplating the significance of Hamelekh Hamishpat, it is readily understandable why the Gemara concluded that one who did not recite the required formula must repeat/return. To interpret the Gemara that it merely requires the mention of Melekh within a phrase that includes Mishpat, even if it does not express the thought of the King sitting on His Throne of Justice to judge mankind, does not appear congruent with having to repeat/return if not mentioned. *

Asseret Yeme Teshubah

It is well established from the writings of the great Sephardic rabbis throughout the centuries that virtually all Sephardic communities until recent times followed Shulhan Arukh on this as on most matters. In addition to the general commitment to Shulhan Arukh, this particular decision reflects the overwhelming majority of classical commentators and decisors including the three pillars of Jewish Law, the Rif (11th C.), the Rambam (12th C.) and the Rosh (13th C.).

Rabbi Yoseph Hayyim, a leading Baghdadian rabbi, in his *Ben Ish Hai* (1898), followed the Ramah. His reason was *safeq berakhot lehaqel* - when there is a doubt if a berakha should be recited we are "lenient" regarding it and omit it, even if we thus depart from Shulhan Arukh. The concept behind this is that we should be extra-careful not to mention the name of the Almighty in vain. For purposes of creating such doubts in the area of pronouncing the Almighty's name, a small minority of opinions should suffice.

This decision has perplexed many rabbis including Hakham Obadiah Yosef. Shall a solitary opinion against a consensus create *safeq berakhot lehaqel* against Shulhan Arukh? Why not depart from Shulhan Arukh on Hamelekh Haqadosh also? Indeed, in that case there is a whole group of classical commentators who instruct not to repeat/return, as described in the second view above. Furthermore, if we follow *safeq berakhot lehaqel* against Shulhan Arukh when there is a small minority of dissenting opinion we would hardly be able to say any berakhot! (Elsewhere, the *Ben Ish Hai* himself recognized this problem in supporting the recital of certain berakhot against small minority opinions.)

Perhaps the most important question raised against viewing this matter as one of *safeq berakhot lehaqel* is that in the case of the amida one cannot indiscriminately apply such a rule. Consider the dilemma. Upon realizing in the middle of the amida that he did not recite the appropriate concluding formula, one would not be able to continue, for how could he recite the following berakhot - perhaps he should return as indicated by the <u>majority</u> view, and if he does not, proceeding onwards would be taking the Almighty's name in vain! Proceeding onwards in this case would transform even the earlier berakhot of the amida to "vain" ones! Obviously, there are self-restricting limitations to being strict.

Although it does not answer the questions, perhaps the *Ben Ish Hai* considered an opinion cited in Ramah's glosses as authoritative as sufficient for invoking *safeq berakhot lehaqel*.

It is evident that our Syrian community practice originally was as stated in Shulhan Arukh. The most authoritative of the post-Shulhan Arukh rabbis accepted by our community, Rabbi Haim Yoseph David Azoulai, (Rab Hida), in Birke Yoseph (1774), the Radbaz, the Pri Hadash, and almost all early Sephardic *posqim*, followed Shulhan Arukh on this. Two famous Syrian-Israeli rabbis of the early 20th Century, Rabbi Yoseph Yedid of Jerusalem and Rabbi Haim Sitton of Safed, concurred. The collection of Halachot assiduously studied by many of our community's learned men this past century, the Bet Obed (1843), also follows Shulhan Arukh on this. The 1885 edition of Selihot brought to press by Rabbi Yishaq Dayan of Aleppo, found in some community old-timers' homes, also follows Shulhan Arukh on this.

It is worthy of note that Rabbi Matloub Abady, a"h, a rabbi in Aleppo before emigrating to the United States, where he was widely recognized as the outstanding rabbinical authority in the American Sephardic community, often

115

stated that the *Ben Ish Hai* was not accepted as authoritative in Aleppo.

In the 1950's, Israeli-published siddurim with brief halakhot entered our community and for many years took over synagogue, school and home. On the Hamelekh Hamishpat issue they followed the *Ben Ish Hai*, so many conducted accordingly. Additionally, the works of the *Ben Ish Hai* and another great Baghdadian rabbi the Kaf Hahayim, who also instructed not to repeat/return, became increasingly popular amongst laymen in the 50's. The entry of non-Syrian rabbis and teachers into the community over the past 40-50 years has also played a role as has the "cross-fertilization" of travelers. These forces influenced many changes in our Aleppo liturgy and customs, but this is not the place for such a discussion.

The Qol Ya`aqob siddur merely informs to recite Hamelekh Hamishpat without instructions in case of omission.

NOTES: * Rabbi Yaacov Schwarz interprets the Ramah as consistent with his position regarding one who recited the amida without concentration (kavana). Shulhan Arukh states that if one did not have *kavana* in at least the first berakha he should repeat the amida. The Ramah disagrees as even the repetition will probably be without *kavana*. The allowance for everybody to recite the amida is itself a concession to maintain the halakha of praying, but it is appropriate to rely on any plausible interpretation to exempt repetition. The reason the Ramah did not follow the minority view on *Hamelekh Haqadosh* is because that controversy is on interpreting the Gemara's language and the indication is clear to all like the majority.

Halakhot of Yom Kippur

I. Overview

G-d created man and instilled in him free will so that man may choose to serve his Creator and abide by His commandments, thereby to be attached to the Divine will. The Torah provides the guidelines.

In general, abiding by G-d's will is defined a number of times throughout Tanakh. G-d praised Abraham because "he will instruct his children and household after him to observe the way of Hashem, to do righteousness and justice..." (Gen. 18:17-19). "What is it the Lord requires of you, only to do *mishpat*, love *ḥesed*, and walk modestly with your G-d" (Micah 6:8). "But let him who chooses to be praised be praised in this, that he understands and knows Me, that I am Hashem who does *ḥesed*, *mishpat* and *sedaqah* in the earth, for in these do I desire, declared Hashem" (Jer. 9:23). "*Ḥesed umishpat* observe" (Hosea 12:7).

Since "there is no man on earth ... who does not sin" (Qohelet 7:20), G-d granted Israel one day each year, the day of Yom Kippur, to facilitate repentance, to purify everyone and grant them forgiveness and atonement. He established this day because He does not desire the death of the sinners, neither physically nor spiritually, but their repenting and living. Indeed, He does not desire the destruction of the world but its flourishing. His desire is that all human society cease from all unethical and immoral behavior and return to Him. It is the responsibility of the nation of Israel to play a leadership role in accomplishing this. Of course, the decision to repent is in the hands of man, dependent on his exercise of his free will.

Halakhot of Yom Kippur

The prohibitions of the day of Yom Kippur, the fasting and other hardships, and the prayers, help us acknowledge the reality that we have sinned, that we have not sufficiently thought about our actions, that there is great need for improvement and that we deserve punishment. Most of our waking hours during the twenty-four hours of Yom Kippur should be devoted to prayer, introspection, repentance (*Teshubah*) and some time should be made for study of Torah.

II. Ereb Yom Kippur

It is proper for each person to ask forgiveness from anyone he/she may have wronged before the day of Kippur sets in. When one wrongfully harmed another monetarily, it is best to settle before Kippur. When not practical, at least the apology and the commitment to settle should be given to the wronged party before Kippur.

It is a mitzvah to eat well Ereb Yom Kippur.

Some have a practice to make symbolic *kaparah* on Ereb Yom Kippur (or during the few days before it) with chickens, one for each member of the family. Some give a donation to charity in place of chickens. Some, following Shulhan Arukh, which specifically and strongly stated that this custom should be eliminated because it looks like the way of idolators, do not engage in this practice at all.

Minha is prayed early so that there should be sufficient time for all to eat and get ready for the holy day before sunset. Talet and tefillin are worn at minha.

After the final berakha of the individual's amida of minha, but before reciting the amida's concluding portion, viduy (acknowledgment and confession of sins) is recited. It is not repeated in hazara.

It is customary to kindle a remembrance candle or a light in or about the synagogue as a memorial for departed members of the family. Remembrance of the departed may serve as inspiration for the living.

It is customary for men to immerse in a mikvah (or natural body of water) on Ereb Kippur with thoughts of repentance and purification in their minds. When one is not available or it is impractical it is appropriate to intend such purification with a shower somewhat longer than usual. Although a shower is invalid for the law of a woman's fulfilling the mitzvah of mikvah after her period, immersing of men is not an actual law.

Se`uda Hamafseket: The final meal before Yom Kippur begins must be completed before sunset, at which time the fast and all halakhot of the day begin. If one completes this meal early it is considered an early acceptance of the fast unless the person stated (or specifically thought) that he/she does not wish to accept the fast yet. When one accepts the fast early, it is understood that all the laws of Yom Kippur take effect for that individual at that time.

Some communities have the custom to light candles before sunset, as before Shabbat and festivals, and some do not. A widespread practice is to light without a berakha.

Men wear a talet for all Yom Kippur prayers, including arbit. One should try to arrive at the synagogue before sunset so as to be able to say the berakha on donning the talet.

The evening service begins with the chanting of *Lecha Keli*. Although the Torah is not read during the evening, the Ark is opened and the Torah is shown to the congregation, to increase the level of inspiration. Seven Torah scrolls are brought out and *Kal Nidre* is recited three times in the past tense and once in the future tense. It is preferable that this be done before nightfall. The berakha of *Sheheheyanu* (for the arrival of Yom Kippur) is recited before beginning arbit.

III. Yom Kippur and Repentance

Since Yom Kippur, the final day of the Ten Days of Repentance that begin with Rosh Hashana, is the time of Teshubah for each individual as well as for the community, each individual is responsible to repent and confess any wrongdoing on this day. The rabbis have formulated comprehensive texts of confession that are incorporated in the prayers of the day. These include *viduy hagadol*, a long list of transgressions. Although this list of transgressions includes some that most people undoubtedly did not commit, it is permitted to be recited by all, as it is considered a communal confession. Also, one may be responsible for a transgression that was committed by another due to having played a role in causing it. The ripple effects of a transgression go far and wide.

Yom Kippur secures atonement only for those who have faith in the power of atonement that G-d placed in the day.

Teshubah and Yom Kippur secure atonement for sins between man and G-d only. For sins against one's fellow man there is no atonement until the penitent has compensated the injured party for any loss and gained his forgiveness. One must seek forgiveness from his fellow man even if he had only angered him with words.

One being asked for forgiveness should not be difficult to appease but rather quick to forgive with a sincere heart (of course not speaking of monetary debts). If the injured party is confident that the person requesting forgiveness is insincere, he is not obliged to grant forgiveness.

It is proper that each individual specifically state at the beginning of the evening of Yom Kippur that he/she forgives everyone (excluding monetary debts).

Just as one must repent of sins involving actions, so must one repent of evil dispositions that he/she may have. These may include a tendency to anger quickly, jealousy, overweening pride, greediness, gluttony, etc.

IV. The Four Components of Repentance

1. *Viduy* - confessional: this is acknowledgment and identification (mention) of the sin. When done silently it is appropriate to specify the particular transgression being repented for.
2. The decision to abandon the sinful practice.
3. Having a feeling of regret for having transgressed.
4. A resolution for the future. In making a resolution, it is proper to devise a strategy to cope with the temptation that may arise and "build a fence" around the transgression.

V. Prohibitions

All work that is forbidden on Shabbat is forbidden on Yom Kippur. The prohibitions specific to Yom Kippur are:

 a) eating and drinking
 b) washing the body
 c) application of ointments to the body
 d) wearing leather shoes
 e) marital relations.

Sick people and women who are pregnant, nursing or who recently gave birth (after the first three days) are not automatically exempt from fasting on Yom Kippur as is the case with the minor fasts. Exemption is based on there being at least a minor possibility that fasting would endanger life. Medical experts have stated that in normal pregnancies there is no danger in fasting, although in the later months it may induce labor. A medical and halakhic authority should be consulted in individual cases.

A woman in labor on Yom Kippur should eat.

One who must eat or drink on Yom Kippur for medical or health reasons should do so in as limited a fashion as possible. If it does not increase the danger to do so, it is proper to eat less than an ounce of food at a time. After the passage of a ten-minute period from having started, the individual may once again eat less than an ounce of food, and repeat this process as often as necessary. Drinking should be limited to one and a half ounces of liquid in a five-minute period. If necessary, the interval for drinking may be just long enough that it is not considered the same drinking.

One who eats or drinks on Yom Kippur does not recite qiddush.

Washing the body on Yom Kippur should be limited to the fingers. *Netilat Yadayim* is up to the knuckles. It is permitted to wipe away the sediment from one's eyes in the morning. After using the bathroom, or if one has touched a covered part of the body, one should wash up to the knuckles. However, if a part of the body became very sweaty or dirty, it is permitted to wash in a limited manner, for the essential prohibition of washing the body is when done for pleasure.

Application of a spray or solid deodorant to prevent body odor is permitted.

An individual who is distressed when not brushing teeth or using mouthwash, may do so in a careful, limited manner.

Non-leather sneakers that have non-structural leather ornamentation are permitted. Leather garments other than shoes are permitted.

VI. Prayers

On both the night and day of Yom Kippur, the phrase *Barukh Shem Kebod Malkhuto Le`olam Va`ed*, is recited audibly upon reciting Shema.

In Birkhot Hashahar, the blessing of *She`asah Li Qol Sorki* is omitted. Although the appreciation expressed in this berakha is general, it was established to be recited in conjunction with the putting on of leather shoes. Since on this day we do not wear such shoes we omit it. On other days, if one does not wear leather shoes, he still recites this berakha as they could be worn and as others are wearing them.

The Torah reading for *shahrit* is the portion that describes the Yom Kippur service in the sanctuary. Another portion about Yom Kippur is read from a second Sefer Torah. The haftarah is the portion from the prophet Yeshaya that criticizes superficial repentance on a fast day, describing true repentance and calling on the nation of Israel to comport ethically.

During hazara (repetition of the amida) of musaf, the hazzan recites the *Aboda,* a description of the Yom Kippur service by the high priest in the days of the Temple. The Ark is opened for this prayer.

Halakhot of Yom Kippur

The Torah reading at minha is the portion exhorting Israel to refrain from immoral conduct, particularly sexual impropriety. The haftarah reading is *Sefer Yonah*, which deals in depth with the subject of repentance and G-d's compassion on all people, even sinners.

The shofar is not blown during Yom Kippur proper; it is blown after sunset toward the conclusion of the day. The blowing of the shofar does not signal the end of the day, as the day continues until the "stars appear," approximately thirty-five minutes after sunset in the New York region.

There are five *amidot* recited on Yom Kippur. In addition to musaf, *ne'ila* is recited after *minha*. This is the "closing" prayer, also so-called in reference to the closing of the Heavenly Gates that are especially opened on Yom Kippur.

The Aron Haqodesh is opened at the beginning of *ne'ila* and is kept open for the duration of this important prayer.

Birkat Kohanim is not recited in minha, but is recited in *ne'ila*. It must be said before sunset.

It is customary to recite "the long viduy" during Yom Kippur. There is a version of the *viduy hagadol* for the positive commandments and a version for the negative ones. Some congregations have the custom to recite the version for the negative precepts in arbit and the version for the positive precepts during musaf.

At the conclusion of Yom Kippur habdalah is recited. The candle must be lit from a flame that was burning all of Yom Kippur and "rested." The berakha on besamim (fragrant spices) is not recited. When Kippur occurs on Shabbat, habdalah may be recited on a candle lit from a fire produced at the moment.

Halakhot of Sukkot

I. Introduction

The festival of Sukkot commemorates the extraordinary care and protection that Hashem bestowed upon the Israelites during their perilous wandering through the wilderness. In the first instance it refers to their travels through the desert upon leaving Egypt. It also reminds us of the special providence Hashem extended Israel through its history traveling through the "Wilderness of the Nations" (Ezek. 20:35). Sukkot is one of the *shalosh regalim*, the three festivals prescribed in the Torah (the other two being Pesah and Shabu`ot), when the members of the nation went to the central sanctuary to celebrate.

The first day of Sukkot and the eighth day, called Shemini Asseret (essentially "a festival for itself" attached to Sukkot), are days of yamim tobim, full festival occasions on which work is prohibited except that connected to *okhel nefesh* (see our Halakhot of Yom Tob). The six intermediate days are hol hamo`ed, that is "non-holy" days of the festival, days on which work may be performed with certain restrictions. In the Diaspora, Sukkot begins with two days of yom tob and concludes with two days yom tob of Shemini Asseret, with five intermediate days.

II. Mitzvah of Sukkah

A commandment of the Torah is to reside in a sukkah all seven days of Sukkot. A sukkah – derived from *sekhakh* (covering) – refers to a booth generally constructed for temporary or modest dwelling, such as might be provided for cattle (Gen. 33:17) or an orchard watchman (Isa. 1:8). The *sekhakh* of the sukkah plays a critical role in determining its halakhic acceptability. Residence primarily comprises eating and sleeping but also includes other

Halakhot of Sukkot

activities one does at home such as reading, resting, social conversation, etc.

The *berakha* recited for this mitzvah is *lesheb basukkah*. Although one performs a mitzvah whenever residing in the sukkah during the seven days of Sukkot, the blessing is not recited except upon partaking of a significant minimum measurement of bread or mezonot.

Less than *kebessa* of bread (the volume of an average egg, see below) may be eaten outside the sukkah; more than that requires a sukkah and the berakha of *lesheb basukkah*.

Cake, crackers, cookies and other baked *mezonot* items may be eaten outside the sukkah as long as one does not eat an amount that is considered having "established a meal" of the mezonot. This measure is considered by some authorities to be the volume of three average eggs, which requires reciting *hamosi*, birkat hamazon and eating in a sukkah with the berakha of *lesheb basukkah*. The volume of four average eggs of such mezonot products definitely requires the above. In practical halakha there is a dispute concerning these measurement; some authorities consider a *kebessa* volume to be approximately two ounces of weight of bread or cake while others consider it to be not more than one and one-third ounces of weight of bread or cake.

In the case of cooked mezonot products such as pasta, when one eats the minimum measure they require sukkah and *lesheb basukkah* despite the fact that they never require the berakhot of *hamosi* and birkat hamazon, but mezonot and *al hamihya*, even when they comprise a "regular" meal.

Fruits, vegetables and drinks are permitted outside the sukkah in any quantity. Whoever is careful to eat and drink in the sukkah even when partaking of less than the minimum measure that requires sukkah is praiseworthy. It is proper to eat mezonot items that are of at least a *kebessa* in the sukkah even though they do not require *lesheb basukkah.*

When reciting the blessings, one first recites *hamosi* then *lesheb basukkah.* On yom tob or Shabbat, since there is *qiddush, lesheb basukkah* is attached to the *qiddush.* If one forgot to recite it at the beginning of his meal, he may do so as long as he is still within the meal, even if he no longer intends to eat bread.

On the first night of Sukkot, one is required to eat at least a *kazzayit* of bread in the sukkah. (*Kazzayit* is dependent on the *kebessa*, but one ounce is surely adequate.) In the Diaspora this applies to the second night also.

There are four berakhot in the *qiddush* of the first two nights of Sukkot: the first is on the wine, the second commemorates the festival, followed by *lesheb basukkah* and *sheheheyanu.* On the second night the order of the third and fourth blessings are reversed as explained below.

The *sheheheyanu* in the *qiddush* on all first nights of festivals expresses gratitude for being alive to fulfill the mitzvah of celebrating the festival. On Sukkot it also applies to the mitzvah of construction of the sukkah (even if the individual reciting the *qiddush* did not build or does not own the sukkah). Therefore, on the first night it is recited after *lesheb basukkah*, to cover both mitzvot. On the second night, *sheheheyanu* is only for the festival, recited because of the "doubt of the day" that used to apply. As far as construction of the sukkah is concerned, the *sheheheyanu* of the first night would cover it even if the first night were not really the festival, as the sukkah was already completed. Although these considerations derive from a situation that no longer obtains today we do not have the authoritative Bet Din to bring the halakha into alignment with the reality.

III. Exemptions From the Mitzvah

Women are not required to eat in the sukkah, as it is one of the positive commandments governed by time from which they are exempt. If they choose to eat in the sukkah they fulfill a mitzvah. However, they should not recite *lesheb basukkah*, as they cannot properly say *vesivanu* ("He commanded us"). This principle applies to all such cases in which women are exempt but choose to fulfill the mitzvah.

In cold or inclement climates one need not sleep in the sukkah. One should not sleep in the sukkah if it is dangerous, for "danger is more serious than a prohibition."

A sick person who is discomforted when eating in the sukkah, even if his illness is not life threatening, is exempt. The sick person's attendant is also exempt.

When it is raining hard enough to interfere with the normal use of the sukkah as a room in one's home, one is exempt and may eat bread outside the sukkah. If, nonetheless, one chooses to eat in the sukkah, he is not allowed to recite the berakha on the sukkah. The rabbis consider a person who does so *hedyot*. Similarly, other adverse conditions in the sukkah that cause one significant discomfort, such as extreme cold or bad odor not under one's control, also exempt one from the sukkah.

If one began his meal indoors because it was raining, and the rain stopped while he was in the midst of the meal, he does not have to move to the sukkah or refrain from bread during the rest of the meal. Once he was exempt at the beginning of the meal he is exempt for the whole meal.

If it rains the first night of Sukkot before one fulfilled the mitzvah of eating in the sukkah, and the individual is prepared to begin his meal, he should wait a half hour or so to see if the rain stops or if there is a sign of stopping. If it does not stop, and there is no sign of stopping, he may then eat with bread in the house. Even the first night there is no mitzvah to eat in the sukkah while disturbed by rain.

However, on the first night, since eating in the sukkah is a specific mitzvah from the Torah, if the rain stopped after one began or completed his meal, he should enter the sukkah to eat at least a measure of bread with the berakha of *lesheb basukkah*. If the rain stopped after one went to bed to sleep for the night, it is not then necessary to go to the sukkah.

Travelers during Sukkot are exempt from sukkah during their journeying times and may eat bread outside a sukkah providing they are traveling for purposes of business or mitzvah. Those traveling for pleasure are not exempt from sukkah and even if a sukkah is not available in their vicinity they should refrain from eating the measure of bread that requires a sukkah.

IV. The Sukkah

A sukkah must be at least ten *tefahim* (handbreadths) high, approximately thirty-five inches. In times past, when it was common to sit on the floor, this height was adequate. The maximum height for a sukkah is twenty *amot* or "cubits" (an average person's forearm, approximately twenty-one inches). Thus, the maximum acceptable height for a sukkah is about 35 feet. If it were higher, an individual sitting in the sukkah might not sense being under the *sekhakh* covering.

Halakhot of Sukkot

A sukkah must have at least two walls and part of a third. In a standard rectangular sukkah, two walls must extend for at least seven *tefahim* each (24½ inches) while the third must extend at least over four *tefahim* (14 inches).

Sukkah walls may be constituted of any material providing they are strong enough to withstand a wind normal for the particular locale during the Sukkot season. The commercial canvas walls common in our times are acceptable providing they are fastened well all along their width on top and bottom. It is preferable they not flutter more than three *tefahim* off center.

The Sukkah must be covered with *sekhakh* that shades the majority of the area of the sukkah.

Sekhakh must be:
a. Of a material that grows from the ground
b. Detached from the ground
c. Able to remain for seven days without decomposing
d. Not subject to the laws of ritual impurity, thus excluding receptacles, vessels and foodstuffs.

The most usual materials for *sekhakh* are bamboo, evergreens and thin wooden slats. It is acceptable to use bamboos spliced into thin strips and interlaced to make a "mat", providing it was made for overhead covering or at least not for a floor mat (which involves a technical point of association with a potential defilement).

Sekhakh should not be so solid that heavy rain cannot penetrate the sukkah. It is preferred to be sufficiently thin so that some stars may be visible from the sukkah.

An air gap in the sekhakh of less than three *tefahim* (10½ in.) does not invalidate the sukkah, but one should not eat under such a gap. Invalid *sekhakh* of less than four *tefahim* (14 in.) in the midst of kosher *sekhakh* does not invalidate the sukkah and one is permitted to eat underneath such a spot. In a minimum-size sukkah (of seven *tefahim*) these two lenient regulations are inapplicable, as there would not be enough space remaining for a kosher sukkah.

An area that extends into the sukkah from a side wall may have invalid *sekhakh* (such as a regular roof) up until four *amot* (seven feet) without invalidating the sukkah. The reasoning is that the part of the ceiling connected to the wall may be considered a continuation of the wall (a curved wall). However, the invalid sekhakh area is not considered part of the sukkah; thus, there must be a minimum size of sukkah without it. When eating in such a sukkah one must be under the valid *sekhakh*.

A sukkah should not be built under any projection (e.g. a ledge, an overhang or trees). If part of the sukkah is under a projection, that part is invalid and one should not eat in that spot.

It is a mitzvah to decorate the sukkah. Decorations may be attached to the *sekhakh* even though the decorations are made of material that is invalid for *sekhakh*. Decorations within four *tefahim* of the *sekhakh* are annulled to it and one may eat under them.

V. The Four Species - Lulab, Etrog, Hadas and Araba

The Torah prescribes to take (lift up) the four species on the first day of Sukkot and rejoice. The Talmud defines these as etrog (citron), lulab (palm branch), hadas (myrtle branches) and araba (willow branches). In the central sanctuary the mitzvah was performed all seven days of Sukkot. The rabbis extended the mitzvah to all seven days everywhere.

131

The mitzvah is performed once daily during daytime only. It is not performed on Shabbat as the rabbis feared it would lead to carrying.

Women are not obligated in this mitzvah as it is a positive mitzvah governed by time. They may choose to perform the mitzvah, but without a berakha.

One lulab, three hadasim and two arabot should be bound together, so that the three species comprise a single unit. It is customary to bind them with lulab leaves. The binding should preferably be done before yom tob so that the binding material can be cut to size and knots made. If it was not done before yom tob, it may be done on yom tob in an inferior manner, without cutting and without proper knots.

In fulfilling the mitzvah, one takes the three species bound together in his right hand, recites the berakha, then takes the etrog in his left hand (even if left-handed) and holds the four species together, and waves them. The central spine of the lulab (*shidra*) should face towards the person. The berakha is recited just before taking the etrog in hand in accordance with the rule that berakhot on mitzvot are recited just before fulfillment. If preferred, one may hold the etrog upside down before the berakha and turn it right side up after the berakha, as the mitzvah is not fulfilled until the four species are held right side up. Right side up means the point of detachment from the tree is to the bottom.

On the first day two berakhot are recited: *al netilat lulab* and *sheheheyanu*. On the rest of the days only the first berakha is recited.

While waving, one should silently request G-d to provide beneficial rains and dew and helpful winds during the coming year. One should have kavana (focused thoughts) for the land of Israel, the country he is in and, in a general way, the world-at-large.

The Torah indicates that we should each take our own set of four species. This applies to the first day (in the Diaspora the first two days). If one does not have his own set, someone may present him with a "gift" with the understanding that it will be returned. If the congregation owns its own set, each member is considered a partner and each is understood to relinquish his share on behalf of whoever wishes to use it.

There is a technical problem involved with the giving of the lulab set to children on the first day. Halakhically, a child can acquire property when an adult gives it to him, but cannot give over property. Therefore, if a child does not have his own set, an adult should be careful not to transfer his to the child as a "gift" on the first day before all the adults who intend to use that set that day have done so.

The lulab must measure at least four *tefahim* (14 in.); hadas and araba stalks must measure at least three *tefahim* each (10½ in.). An etrog must be at least the volume of an average egg.

An etrog from which even a small amount is missing is invalid. This includes the node from which the *pitum* protrudes. Etrogim that grow naturally without such a node are acceptable. The upper portion of an etrog (the upper slope until the top) should be very presentable, without flaws such as discoloration or "scales." Flaws on the lower portion of the etrog are not as serious and its acceptability depends on the extent.

Proper hadas has three or more leaves protruding from the same horizontal line all along its stem. At the minimum, it should be "tripled" for at least four and one-half inches along its stem, which is the majority of the *bedi'avad* measurement of hadas. If all the leaves dry up to the extent that they no longer are green but "whitish," it is invalid.

Proper araba has smooth-edged leaves. If the majority of the leaves dry up or fall off, it is invalid.

Whatever is invalid because of "missing," poor appearance or blemishes is only invalid the first day.

Hadas and particularly araba spoil relatively quickly. To preserve them, it is helpful to wrap them in a large sheet of aluminum foil, wet newspaper or a damp towel and refrigerate.

A halakhic principle is to "beautify the mitzvot." As the etrog is defined as the Biblical *hadar*, it is especially appropriate to seek an especially presentable etrog.

VI. Shemini Asseret

The festival of the eighth day (and the ninth day in the Diaspora), Shemini Asseret, is a separate festival in many respects. Thus, the halakhot of sukkah and the "four species" do not apply to it.

It is customary to eat in the sukkah on the first day of Shemini Asseret without reciting the berakha on the sukkah. This is based on the practice of conducting as they did before establishment of a set calendar, when they had the doubt regarding the day, i.e. perhaps the eighth day is really the seventh day and still Sukkot.

The reason we do not recite the berakha on sukkah because of the "doubt" that they had is that in the evening it would be recited in the *qiddush*, thus creating a totally inappropriate situation: we would mention Shemini Asseret and explicitly contradict our declaration with the blessing of *lesheb basukkah*. Merely sitting in the sukkah, however, does not create a contradiction as we may choose to eat outdoors independently of the festival.

However, since we now know the day is Shemini Asseret and there is no requirement to sit in the sukkah, slight discomfort permits eating indoors, as the mitzvah to be joyous in celebrating the festival is from the Torah and the custom to comport in accordance with the "doubt of the day" that they had before the set calendar cannot override it.

We begin reciting *mashib haru'ah umorid hageshem* in the amida of musaf of Shemini Asseret. If one mistakenly recited *morid hatal* he does not repeat, as dew is appropriate all year long. We do not begin *barekh alenu* in the amida (that includes the *tal umatar* request for rain) until December 4th or 5th.

VII. Simhat Torah

Simhat Torah is celebrated on Shemini Asseret; in the Diaspora it is celebrated on the second day. On this day we conclude the reading of the Torah and begin reading it anew. It is then appropriate to focus our intentions on increasing our study of the Torah this time around.

We read from three *Sifre Torah*. In the first we conclude the Torah, in the second we begin Beresheet and in the third we read the maftir for the day. Although we normally recite *qaddish* after a required reading of each Sefer Torah of yom tob or Shabbat, the custom is not to recite *qaddish* after concluding the Torah so as not to interrupt between concluding it and beginning it again.

Three *hatanim* (grooms of the Torah) are designated for the readings. The *Hatan Me`ona* reads the portion of the Torah that precedes the concluding portion, the *Hatan Torah* concludes, while the *Hatan Beresheet* begins from the beginning of the Torah.

It is customary to give many aliyot on this day, including to children to increase their love for the Torah. Very young children are sent up in groups with an older child leading them in the berakha. The extra aliyot are generally given before the aliya of *Hatan Me`ona*, although some have the custom to send up the *Hatan Me`ona* as hamishi (before the extra aliyot).

A special celebration is made in honor of the Torah. The rabbis and the public dance with the Torah and circle the Torah seven times with singing and dancing both at night and by day. If indicated, it is permitted to take the Sefer Torah outdoors to increase the celebration.

VIII. Prayers

*Ya`ale veyabo* is recited in each amida. If it was omitted during the intermediate days (hol hamo`ed, when a weekday amida is recited), and the individual did not realize it until having concluded, he repeats the amida, for he made no mention of the special day. If he realized the omission before concluding the amida, he should return to *rese* and repeat from that point on, which includes *ya`ale veyabo*. On yom tob, if mention of the festival was made in the amida independently of *Ya`ale Veyabo*, one does not need to repeat.

Complete Hallel with a berakha is recited after the amida of *shahrit* each day for all nine days. The lulab set is waved in all six directions on each of the days of Sukkot except

Halakhot of Sukkot

Shabbat (that is, on six days) during the recital of certain verses in Hallel. While waving, one should silently pray for a year of adequate rain and dew.

Hosha'not are recited daily for the seven days of Sukkot after Hallel. A Sefer Torah is placed on the tebah and each individual circles around it while holding a set of the four species. Our custom is to bring the Sefer Torah to the tebah before *Barukh She'amar*. On Shabbat, as the four species are proscribed, Hoshanot are not recited. Some recite Hoshanot composed especially for Shabbat but do not bring out a Sefer Torah for it.

Specified selections are read from the Torah each morning. The minimum number of aliyot on yom tob is five plus maftir. The number of aliyot on hol hamo'ed is four.

Each day of Sukkot, before arbit and in the morning prayers, we recite Psalms 42 and 43 that connect to the theme of the occasion. For Shemini Asseret we recite Psalm 12.

Musaf is said daily.

The last day of hol hamo'ed is *Hosh'anah Rabbah*. There is a custom to stay up all night and read the complete books of Debarim and Tehillim. We pray for one more chance.

On Hoshanah Rabbah seven sections of hosh'anot are recited, during each of which the congregants circle the Sefer Torah on the tebah.

At the conclusion of musaf, five arabot, bound together, are beaten five times on the ground with a silent prayer that G-d should grant us a year during which the earth yields its produce abundantly.

Halakhot of Sukkot

Tefillin are not donned for all nine days.

Ya`ale veyabo is recited in birkat hamazon throughout the festival including the intermediate days.

Regarding the Date to Begin Reciting Tal Umatar

I. Introduction

In the second blessing of the musaf prayer of Shemini Asseret, a blessing that constitutes recitation of various manifestations of the Deity's might, we begin reciting *"mashib haru'ah umorid hageshem"*, "Who drives the wind and brings down the rain." This is merely a *mention* of rain in our prayers, not a formal request. This mention continues until the first day of Pesah. As Shemini Asseret (Tishri 22) falls about the time when rain is required in Israel, the rabbis established it as the appropriate occasion to begin reciting Hashem's praise concerning this detail of His power. It is important to recognize that this is not a *request* for rain but rather a *praise* of Hashem.

Recital of the request prayer for rain, *veten tal umatar librakha*, "and grant dew and rain for blessing," is incorporated in the ninth berakha of the weekday amida, *Barekh Alenu*, and was deferred for two weeks until Heshvan 7. The rabbis deemed it appropriate to allow those who came to Jerusalem for the Sukkot festival from distant locations to return home before everybody began requesting rain, which, were it to fall, would be an inconvenience for travelers. This is in Israel. Although the reasons do not apply today, the *taqana* to begin this prayer at that time remains.

The Diaspora, which in Talmudic times was primarily Babylonia and nearby lands, did not require rain as early as did Israel. So the *taqana* differentiated and established that in the Diaspora - though they should begin the praise of Hashem concerning rain on Shemini Asseret - the request

139

for rain should begin sixty days after the *Tequfa* (the autumn equinox). Many *posqim*, followed by Shulhan Arukh, apply the sixty-day regulation even to distant lands. Although the Diaspora in Talmudic times spread over a relatively limited area and not all the many variations as to when rain was required in the much expanded Diaspora could be subsumed in the category of 60 days after the equinox, that was all that was explicitly established for it in the early *taqana*. This has engendered many interesting issues through the centuries but that is not our topic here.

II. Calendar Problems

According to the Bet Yosef, in the Diaspora the equinox day itself is counted as Day One and Tal Umatar is to begin in arbit of the 60th day.

The autumn equinox, dependent on the solar cycle, occurs September 23rd in our civil calendars in use today except during leap years, when it occurs September 22nd. Were a precise calendar used for Tal Umatar purposes today, the 60th day from the equinox would be November 21st, and during leap years, November 20th. However, for purposes of calculating the seasons when dealing with rabbinical law such as in our case, the convenient formula given by the third century Talmudic sage Shemuel was used, in contrast to calendrical calculations that directly affect Torah law which are based on the more precise formula of another third century Talmudic sage, Rab Adda (whose calculations were also in discrepancy with the actual length of the year but much less so).

Shemuel stated that there are 91 days and 7 1/2 hours between season and season, each of which he thought to be equal to exactly one fourth of a year, which he thought to be comprised of 365 days and 6 hours. (This very possibly had originally only been intended as a rule-of-thumb guideline.) Rab Adda's solar year comprised 365 days 5 hours 55 minutes and 25 seconds. The actual value of the length of a year, determined centuries later, is 365 days, 5 hours, 48 minutes and 46 seconds. The annual discrepancy between the longer solar year of Shemuel and the precise astronomical year is 11 minutes 14 seconds. The accumulated difference since Shemuel's time in the mid-third century - let us say the year 250 of the common era - until the year 2000 totals a bit more than 13 1/2 extra days. 11.23 min x 1750 yrs = 19653 min / 1440 min per day = 13.6 days

In accordance with Shemuel, that means to say, incorporating this discrepancy, at the start of the 21st Century (as was also the case in the 20th Century) the traditional practice was to begin reciting Tal Umatar December 4th at night (or December 5th according to some opinions, as we shall soon explain) except for once every four years when we begin one day later, for a reason that will soon become clear, a total of 13 or 14 days beyond the "60 days after the autumn equinox.."

In Halakhic works written before the year 1582 of our civil calendar, whenever the author provided a Western civil calendar date for Tal Umatar, the date given is many days earlier than the civil calendar dates we use today. About 1555, the Bet Yosef Orah Hayim 117 quoted Rabbi David Abudirham, from a work published in 1340, that for three out of each four years we begin reciting Tal Umatar November 22nd at night and each fourth year November 23rd. This variation resulted from the difference between the civil calendar - termed the Julian Calendar, established by Julius Caesar in 46 B.C.E. - that was in use prior to and during the Bet Yosef's time, who passed away in 1575, and the one in use today.

Until 1582, the Julian Calendar was in use throughout most of the Western World. It was based on a solar year of 365 days and 6 hours, identical with that of Shemuel. In this calendar, three out of every four years were comprised of 365 days and the fourth year (a leap year) was to have one extra day to compensate for the four quarter-days that had not been counted in the span of four years. It was then widely recognized that this calendar contained an error and was "lengthening" the year (which means more leap years were being added than appropriate) in comparison to the actual astronomical year, which by then had been measured very close to its actual value. The start of new years was being delayed by about one day every 128 years.

The Church in Rome acknowledged this discrepancy as a major problem. Its festival calendar - established in 325 - was dependent on the spring equinox and celebrations were falling out of alignment with reality. As years were beginning later and later, the calculated day for the equinox was falling further and further beyond its actual occurrence. In 1582, the equinox was correctly observed as occurring on what is now called March 21st, but the calendar then read March 10th! A full ten-day discrepancy had set in from 325. Later that year, Pope Gregory XIII corrected for the previous 1257 years by changing the date of the day after October 4, 1582, calling it October 15th, thus compensating for the cumulative ten-day error.

Additionally, the pope provided a calendar refinement for the future. As the discrepancy was one day every 128 years, or three days every 384 years, the new Gregorian calendar eliminated three leap years every 400 years. Each fourth year was to remain a leap year as previously (year numbers divisible by four) except for century years not divisible by 400, which would be regular years. (Thus, the years 1700, 1800 and 1900 were not leap years, but 2000 was.) This

Tal Umatar

calendar was still not perfect, but the discrepancy was merely one day every 3,300 years.

The ritual Jewish calendar of course did not adopt these reforms as halakha could not be modified by a decision of the outside world.

III. Civil Date of the Jewish Calendar

Back to the Bet Yosef. In 1555, before the Gregorian Calendar was established, civil calendar dates used by the Jewish community - which are merely convenience applications of the Hebrew ritual calendar - were ten days earlier than the civil dates given for 1582. Thus, the November 22nd date of R. Abudirham became December 2nd. In 1582 the Jewish community began Tal Umatar on that civil date, 10 days "later" on the civil calendar than usual, reflecting the ten days that had been skipped on that calendar. In subsequent years that new civil date held, for the Jewish calendar continued its calculations of 365 and ¼ days as usual.

1600 was a leap year in the Gregorian calendar so in the 17th Century no further adjustment to the civil date was necessary for beginning Tal Umatar, as leap years each four years take care of themselves in the halakha as we shall soon explain. However, 1700, 1800 and 1900 (not divisible by 400) were not leap years. They had to be accounted for in the Jewish calendar's transposing its dates to civil dates by permanently adding a compensatory day for each of those century years. Hence, in each of those centuries the Jewish community began the recital of Tal Umatar one day later than the previous century. This yields December 5th (and Dec. 6th every fourth year) as the primary date for Tal Umatar in the 20th and 21st centuries according to Rabbi Abudirham and apparently also according to the Bet Yosef,

Tal Umatar

who cites him authoritatively. This is one day later than the widely accepted 20th-21st Century practice of December 4/5 (which will hold until the year 2100 arrives, a year not scheduled to be a leap year). Some contemporary sources do consider the December 5/6 dates as authoritative but they are a minority.

There are different possibilities as to exactly how this one-day difference came about. Perhaps the Bet Yosef truly espoused November 22/23 in his days and would have advocated December 5/6 for the 20th-21st Century, and the present-day practice of the majority is not in accordance with him, unusual as that may be. Or perhaps he cited Rabbi Abudirham's dates without comment, assuming he transposed the dates correctly, as he was not very familiar with the non-Jewish civil calendar. The dates were close and looked right so he cited them, but had he carefully looked into them perhaps he would have disagreed by one day. The latter is a strong possibility as will now be shown.

In a passage not quoted by the Bet Yosef, Rabbi Abudirham specifically states, "the 60th day is considered as before 60." In other words, Tal Umatar is not recited until the day following the 60th day. This statement, found in present editions of his work and in the 1740 Amsterdam edition, is not in accordance with the latest decision recorded in the relevant Talmudic passage (BT Ta'anit 10a), which clearly states that the 60th day is considered as after 60. (Perhaps Rabbi Abudirham had a variant reading of that passage.) The Bet Yosef, in a separate paragraph, citing the Talmud, counts the 60th day as after 60, despite his citing without comment the civil date as given by Rabbi Abudirham.

In any event, following our Talmudic text, the majority practice has been to begin Tal Umatar one day prior to the civil date that derives from Rabbi Abudirham.

144

IV. Leap Year Considerations

The considerations involved in beginning Tal Umatar one day later each fourth year (a year not identical with the civil calendar's leap year), just for that year, and not having to begin Tal Umatar one day earlier during civil leap years, follow. In accordance with the tradition of Rabbi Yehoshuah we consider Creation as having occurred in Nissan (the first month of the Torah calendar, March - April) and the first spring equinox as having occurred with the creation of the sun at the beginning of the fourth day. On the spring equinox, day and night are equal. As halakha days begin from the evening we consider the creation of the sun as having occurred in Year One on Tuesday evening 6 p.m. Counting twice 91 days 7 1/2 hours, in accordance with Shemuel's formula, to arrive at the autumn equinox (Tishri, the seventh month in the Torah calendar), brings us 182 days 15 hours later. The time of day of that Tishri equinox would be 9 a.m. Although we consider Creation occurring in Nissan, we count years from Tishri according to the tradition of Rabbi Eliezer. The 9 a.m. Tishri equinox, as far as the count of years is concerned, is in Year Two.

The six hours each solar year possesses beyond the 365 whole days now comes into play. This creates a six-hour yearly movement advancing the time of day when the new year arrives and sun and earth return to the identical relationship of the previous year. Thus, in Year Three the autumn equinox is considered as having occurred at 3 p.m., in Year Four at 9 p.m. and so on. Since every fourth year the equinox falls after nightfall, Tal Umatar is moved to the next day in the solar cycle. This may be viewed as a "Tal Umatar Leap Year," whereby one day is added to compensate for the four quarter-days of four years. It always occurs in Hebrew years whose number is divisible by four. We then continue counting according to Shemuel

Tal Umatar

from that later date but as the civil calendar in use today has a leap year several months following our moving to the next day, we are set back one day and return to the earlier date for the next three years and no further problem is presented by the leap year. As the year 2100 will not be a leap year, the Jewish calendar - if no significant correction is made by a national Bet Din by then - will call for Tal Umatar one day later than the present practice.

V. On the Discrepancy

Regarding the discrepancy between our calculations and the true solar year: The Talmudic sages who established our calendar were undoubtedly aware that a discrepancy of several minutes per year might exist. Just as previously the rabbis had corrected problems in their solar-lunar calibrations by direct observation, they unquestionably expected any significant discrepancy to be corrected by direct observation and improved calculations. They surely were committed to halakha remaining harmonized with reality.

Of course the problems are much more far-reaching. For purposes of intercalating the lunar and solar cycles and establishing festival dates we use the less inaccurate calendar of Rab Adda, but nonetheless our halakha year is longer than the actual. Pesah is slowly drifting forward from the spring equinox month toward the second month of spring. For further details see our study *Basic Structure of the Jewish Calendar*. Hopefully a national Bet Din will one day soon make adjustments based on astronomical observation.

[Please Note: In 2005 and 2006, according to the majority view, Tal Umatar is scheduled to begin December 4th at night. The next Hebrew year divisible by 4 is 5768, so in

2007 Tal Umatar is scheduled to begin December 5th at night and in 2008 will return to December 4th.]

Endnotes

i How communities in countries that have need for rain before sixty days pass from the equinox should conduct has been a topic of lively discussion and debate through the centuries. A number of leading authorities, most notably the Rosh (13th C.), tried but failed to align the practice with the reality.

ii Although a thirteen day delay in reciting the classic prayer for rain is significant, particularly in regions where rain is desperately required earlier, and although it is uncomfortable to be out of harmony with reality to such a great degree, the prevailing opinion has been that without a national Bet Din such an halakhic adjustment cannot be made.

iii Encyclopedia Judaica vol. 5 p. 47; Rabbi Adin Steinzalt's *Eeyunim* to BT Ta`anit 10.

iv If it transpires that the "before 60" text in R. Abudirham is a scribal error, it may be that he *began* counting the 60 days after the equinox, according to the simple translation of the Talmud "60 days *after* the equinox," not counting the equinox day as Day One as the Bet Yosef does.

v BT Rosh Hashana 11a

vi In the Talmud (BT Shabbat 75a) a sage expounds the Biblical statement "for it is your wisdom and insight in the eyes of the nations" (Deut. 4:6) as prescribing a mitzvah to have the knowledge of astronomy, to calculate seasons and constellations.

אמר רבי שמואל בר נחמני אמר רבי יוחנן: מנין שמצוה על האדם לחשב
תקופות ומזלות - שנאמר (דברים ד) ושמרתם ועשיתם כי היא חכמתכם
ובינתכם לעיני העמים איזו חכמה ובינה שהיא לעיני העמים - הוי אומר זה
חישוב תקופות ומזלות.

147

Halakhot of Hanukkah

I. Nerot Hanukkah

1. The eight days of Hanukkah were established by the rabbis as days of happiness and praise-giving to the Almighty in celebration of the miraculous victory of the Macabees and the rededication of the holy Temple in Jerusalem. However, they are not commemorated as yom tob days of the Torah. Thus, working is permitted, festive meals are not required and most mourning laws are applicable. Eulogies are not said except for a hakham at the time of his funeral in his presence'. The holiday's unique mitzvah is kindling Nerot (lights). The fulfillment of happiness' is left for each individual and family to define.

2. Both men and women are obligated in Nerot Hanukkah. Although a positive mitzvah governed by time, women were not exempt; as they played an active role in the miracle they should be active in its commemoration.

3. One menorah is lit per family which covers all the members of the family even those not present. The head of household lights the first candle each night (as that constitutes the primary mitzvah). It is customary for wife and children to light the later candles, in age order.

4. On the first night one cup of oil or one candle is kindled in addition to the shamosh (server). Each successive night another light is added until the eighth night when eight cups of oil or candles are lit. The shamosh is placed to a side, out of alignment with the lights of mitzvah. It is customary to set the shamosh in place before beginning the kindling and kindle it after the last cup or candle of mitzvah. The mitzvah cannot be fulfilled with an electric menorah according to many leading authorities.

148

Halakhot of Hanukkah

Some communities have a custom to light an extra candle to commemorate a later miracle that occurred during Hanukkah. To prevent confusion, such an extra candle should be placed to the side.

5. The cup or candle added each evening should be to the left hand side of the person facing the menora. The new addition is kindled first each evening so that lighting proceeds in a right-hand direction (from left to right).

6. The menorah must contain enough oil or wax at the time of lighting to remain lit at least thirty minutes. It must be set in a place where the flames will not be blown out by a usual breeze or draft or anticipated occurence. If there is a reason to do so, one may extinguish the flames after thirty minutes.

7. The act of lighting nerot that are expected to remain lit for the necessary time span comprises the mitzvah. Thus, if an unanticipated occurrence did extinguish the flames before thirty minutes passed, it is not mandatory to light again. However, it is appropriate to relight without a Berakha.

8. The menorah should be placed by a window facing the street where passersby can see it, to fulfill the mitzvah of publicizing the miracle (*pirsumeh nissa*). In areas of mild climate, it is placed in the open doorway, opposite the mezuzah. It should be placed not below three and not above thirty feet from the ground and where it is going to remain the minimum thirty minutes. If one is in a place where there is legitimate fear of provoking hostility, the menorah may be lit where it cannot be seen from the outside.

9. The proper time to light the nerot (except on Friday) is at *Set Hakokhavim* (the appearance of stars), which in New York is approximately 25-35 minutes after sunset. In

149

rabbinical mitzvot such as Ner Hanukkah the more lenient time measure may be used. *Bedi`avad* (normally meaning 'after it was done', but sometimes, as here, also referring to a case when one is pressed) one may light the nerot from sunset and when necessary even from a short time before sunset. In the latter case one must be sure the oil or candles are sufficient to remain lit for thirty minutes after *set hakokhabim bedi`avad*, one may light all night long with berakhot providing there are passersby on the street, but the sooner the better.

10. Under normal circumstances, to prevent possibly forgetting the mitzvah, one should not begin dinner or begin work on an extended task within the half hour before the proper time to light the menorah. It is customary to pray arbit before lighting.

11. On Friday evening, the menorah is lit before the Shabbat candles. As it must remain lit for a half hour after nightfall and must be lit at least several minutes before sunset, it must contain enough oil or large enough candles to remain lit for over an hour. (Shabbat candles, with ends shaved to fit the menorah, are suitable.) If it happens that a family is lighting close to sunset, after the first Hanukkah light is lit (the essential mitzvah) the woman may turn away from the Hanukkah lighting to light the Shabbat candles.

12. On Saturday night, in the synagogue, Hanukkah lighting is before habdalah. The one who lights relys on having said *Ata Honantanu* in the amida to permit him to do melakha. Although the congregants also recited *Ata Honantanu*, they do not have to do any melakha at that moment, so it is preferable to delay the formal exiting of Shabbat for them - a symbol of our love of Shabbat. In the home, Hanukkah lighting is after habdalah.

13. On the first evening, three berakhot are recited, just prior to lighting: *Lehadlik Ner Hanukkah*; *She`asah Nissim*; *Sheheheyanu*. On subsequent evenings, only the first two are recited. After the first candle is lit all present begin reciting 'Hanerot Halalu' and *Mizmor Shir Hanukkat Habayit*. It is customary to sing Hanukkah songs.

14. The light of the candles, except for that of the shamosh, is to be exclusively for mitzvah and may not be used for any other purpose. If a candle goes out, it must be relit with a match or with the shamosh, but not with one of the menorah candles.

15. Women have the custom not to work for the half hour that the candles are required to remain lit. As they usually have household chores, not working provides opportunity to appreciate the mitzvah and heightens consciousness that the candles are not lit for personal use.

16. It is customary to light a menora each evening between minha and arbit in synagogues with berakhot. If possible, the synagogue menorah should be placed on a Southern wall as a remembrance to the menorah of the Bet Hamiqdash which was on the South side in the *hekhal*. The berakhot in the synagogue are recited only if ten people are present.

17. The lighting in a synagogue may not substitute for the mitzvah to light at home even for the one who did the lighting, even if he is lighting at home only for himself. [In this latter case, since when he lights at home there is no household he is covering, he should only recite the first Berakha (*Lehadliq*). As he personally recited *She`asah Nissim* (and if its the first night, *Sheheheyanu*) in his synagogue lighting, he fulfilled his private obligation as far as those berakhot are concerned.]

II. Regarding One Sleeping Away From Home

1. One who is single and regularly lives with his parents, is covered with their lighting even if he is not present. If a husband is away, his wife lights at home for the family and covers him. If one's family is not lighting at home for whatever reason, he should light with berakhot wherever he is.

2. If one's wife is visiting her parents while he is away and lighting with them, since she is not lighting in the capacity of her own household, he should light with berakhot wherever he is.

3. Even if one is in a time zone that is so different from his family's that the family will not have lit by the time it becomes morning for him, he should not light with a Berakha where he is. He still is included in their lighting.

4. If one is in a place where he will not see nerot Hanukkah at all during a night of Hanukkah if he does not himself light, he should light even though he normally would be included in the lighting of his family.

5. Regarding one not covered by parents or spouse who is a sleeping guest in someone's home: if he eats at his own expense, he is not covered by his host and is obligated to light. Preferably, he should pay a token fee to become a partner in the host's oil or candle and join in with him. If he is a house guest for eating also, such that he pays nothing for the hospitality, he is covered by the lighting of his host as he is presently part of the household.

III. Prayers

1. All eight days *Al Hanissim* and *Beeme Matitya* are added to all the amidot and to birkat hamazon. If one forgot to recite them he does not repeat.

2. Complete Hallel is recited all eight days with a Berakha. Women do not say the berakha. There is no musaf during the regular days of Hanukkah. *Tahanun* (ana) is not said. Tefillin are worn and all other prayers are recited as usual.

3. On all eight days Torah selections about the Mishkan dedication are read from Sefer Bemidbar, Parashat Naso to reflect the rededication of the Second Temple that took place during Hanukkah. On Shabbat this selection is read from a second Sefer Torah as Maftir.

4. Rosh Hodesh Tevet always falls on the sixth day of Hanukkah. Sometimes day 7 is also Rosh Hodesh. (This is one of the two months whose Rosh Hodesh fluctuates between one and two days.)

5. The Haftara for Shabbat Hanukkah (even when Rosh Hodesh) is the prophecy of Zechariah IV:6, regarding the meaning of the Menorah. When there is a second Shabbat during Hanukkah the Haftara is the portion discussing the construction of the Menorah in the First Temple (I Kings 7).

6. When Rosh Hodesh Tevet falls on Shabbat, we read from three *Sifre Torah*. *Qaddish* is surely recited on the second and third; if there were seven aliyot to the first Torah, *Qaddish* is also recited on it.

153

IV. Historical Perspective

In 336 B.C.E. Alexander the Great assumed the throne of Greece. He conquered neighboring lands and actively spread Greek ideals throughout his kingdom. For the next 300 years Greek culture (Hellenism) dominated a large portion of the world, from Western Europe through Persia to the border of India.

Hellenistic Culture was polytheistic; it placed the private individual's pleasure and search for happiness above all other goals. It was antithetical to Judaism, which is based on Monotheism and stresses the individual's responsibilities above his pleasures. By 175 B.C.E., when Antiochus IV assumed the mighty Seleucid throne (ruling over that portion of Alexander's kingdom covering most of the Middle East), Hellenism had permeated most of the vast Greek kingdom. Antiochus recognized that Judaism was incongruent with his kingdom's culture and decided to Hellenize the Jews. He banned Torah study and fulfillment of mitzvot; he had the Bet Hamiqdash defiled, forcing upon it idol worship and pig sacrifices; he placed the death penalty on those who defied the new order.

A courageous group of Jews, led by Matatyahu the Hashmonean and his sons, rose in armed revolt against this anti-Torah regime. In 165 B.C.E. the war culminated in a miraculous victory for the Jews, under the leadership of Yehuda Hamaccabee, the son of Matatyahu. As it says in *Al Hanisim*, the Almighty "delivered the many into the hands of the few...the disbelievers into the hands of those engaged in the Torah." The Bet Hamiqdash was purified and the altar rededicated.

The Talmud relates that when the Jews searched for pure oil with which to light the Menorah in the Bet Hamiqdash,

154

they found one cruse with the Kohen Gadol's seal, containing an amount sufficient for one day's kindling. Miraculously, the small amount of oil sufficed for eight days, until they were able to crush olives and produce pure oil.

Hanukkah, commemorating both the miraculous military victory and the rededication of the purified Temple, is celebrated by lighting a Menorah. This is the symbol for the ascendancy of the spiritual principle over the material. As G-d stated to the prophet Zechariah (6th Century B.C.E.) to be communicated to the national leader Zerubabel - who was reestablishing the Temple and Israel - in explication of a menorah vision: "Not by might nor by strength but by My spirit said the Lord" (4:6).

Halakhot of Purim

I. Overview

Subsequent to the destruction of the First Temple in Jerusalem by the Babylonians (586 B.C.E.) the Persians defeated the Babylonians in war (538 B.C.E.) and became the ascendant power in the Middle East. The northern tribes of Israel had already been exiled by the Assyrians in 722 B.C.E. Most of the remaining remnant of Israel, essentially the tribe of Judah together with Benjamin, had been exiled from the land of Israel by the Babylonians and now lived in the huge Persian Empire. The setting of Megillat Esther is in the city of Shushan, capital of Persia, during the time period between the Babylonian exile and the Return to Zion (later during that sixth century B.C.E., perhaps 516 B.C.E.). The megilla contains an account of a major attempt during that epoch to annihilate the Jewish people, men, women and children, undertaken by Haman, chief advisor to King Ahashverosh. In a beautiful narrative it describes Esther's ascension to becoming queen, Haman's reason for his diabolic intent (the steadfast refusal of Mordekhai, a Jewish leader, to bow to him), details of the decree, and the amazing confluence of events including Queen Esther's intervention that brought about the miraculous saving of the Jewish People. Their extraordinary victory over their enemies was achieved on the fourteenth and fifteenth days of Adar, days ever since celebrated as Purim.

II. Prior to Purim

1. On the Shabbat before Rosh Hodesh Adar, or on Rosh Hodesh Adar itself when it falls on Shabbat, we read Parashat Sheqalim. After the regular Torah reading for that day, we read about the past requirement of contributing a half-sheqel, originally toward construction of the Mishkan,

and subsequently toward the service performed in it, later transposed to that of the Temple. Since Haman proposed to pay ten thousand sheqalim to the king's treasury to destroy the Jewish people, this mitzvah has been seen as symbolizing our intentions to counteract the negative intentions of the enemies of the nation.

2. On the Shabbat immediately before Purim, after the regular Torah reading, we read Parashat Zakhor. This portion calls upon Israel to remember what Amaleq did to us upon our leaving Egypt, while we were traveling in the desert, fatigued and weary. Unprovoked, Amaleq perpetrated evil acts against Israel, specifically attacking the stragglers and weak, having no fear of G-d. We are told to eliminate Amaleq - understood to represent evil-doers - from the world. (On Shabbatot following Purim we read Parashat Parah and Parashat Hahodesh.)

3. Adar 13, usually the day before Purim, is Ta`anit Esther, a day commemorating the fast the Jewish People observed, according to tradition, to prompt repentance when battling their enemies. When Purim falls on Sunday, the fast is observed on the Thursday before, Adar 11.

4. From the entry of the month of Adar, anticipating the coming of Purim, to be followed by Pesah, we increase joyousness and happy events.

5. One going on a trip to where he does not expect to find a megilla, should try to take a megilla with him. If not practical, he may read the megilla from Rosh Hodesh Adar onwards, but without a berakha. Nevertheless, the other mitzvot of Purim should be fulfilled on Purim day.

III. Reading of the Megilla

1. Both men and women are required to read or hear the megilla from a kosher megilla scroll twice on Purim, once at night and again during the day.

2. The mitzvah of reading the megilla is more properly fulfilled in the presence of a congregation in order to participate in publicizing the miracle (*pirsume nissa*). If one cannot come to the synagogue or otherwise participate in a minyan, he/she may read it or hear it read individually.

3. **Berakhot**: Three blessings are recited on the megilla prior to the evening reading:

   a) *Al Miqra Megilla* (for the reading itself)
   b) *She'asah Nissim La'abotenu* (mentioning the miracles Hashem performed for our fathers)
   c) *Sheheheyanu* (expressing gratitude that Hashem has kept us alive to participate in this occasion).

One blessing is recited at the conclusion of the reading, *Harab et Ribenu* (acknowledging that it was Hashem who fought our battles).

The same blessings are recited for the daytime reading except for *Sheheheyanu*. If one omitted *Sheheheyanu* in the evening it should be recited in the day.

4. The berakhot before the reading are recited even when the megilla is being read individually (that is to say, without a minyan), whereas the berakha at the conclusion of the reading is only recited in a minyan.

5. The same berakhot are also to be recited by or for women who are reading or hearing the reading without a

minyan. If ten women are hearing the reading together, although it does not constitute a 'minyan' for other rituals, it is *pirsume nissa* and the concluding berakha is also recited.

6. One holding a kosher megilla scroll may read along with the hazzan. One who does not have a kosher megilla scroll should not read along but listen to every word said by the hazzan and have in mind to fulfill his/her obligation. It is important the hazzan be one who enunciates each word clearly.

7. Every person who reads Hebrew should preferably have at least a printed text of the megilla in front of him/her to follow along quietly. If one misses some of the words read by the hazzan, it is permitted to read them from the printed text and catch up providing this is only done with a minority of the megilla.

8. From the recitation of the first berakha until the conclusion of the last berakha there should be no talking or interruptions. Stamping feet during the reading is disturbing and inappropriate and should not be done. Very young children or those with noise-making toys, who will possibly create a disturbance and interfere with the fulfillment of the mitzvah, should not be present in the synagogue during megilla reading. If such children are in the synagogue, a baby-sitter should be provided in another area.

9. Unlike the case with the Torah, it is permissible to directly touch the megilla scroll when reading (with clean hands of course).

10. Since in the megilla the text is termed a "letter," it is a widespread custom that as a page is read it is not immediately rolled up as is the case with a Torah scroll. At

the conclusion of the reading it is rolled up before beginning the concluding blessing.

11. The time for reading the megilla in the evening begins at *set hakokhabim* (the appearance of stars), the time that the fast ends. One should not eat until performing the mitzvah. As the day concluding with *set hakokhabim* is usually Ta`anit Esther, it may be that one is hungry or thirsty. If necessary, one may have a light snack before the reading.

IV. Mahasit Hasheqel

It is customary to give a half-sheqel or half-dollar to charity for each family member before or on Purim, in commemoration of the mitzvah of *mahasit hasheqel*.

V. Mishlo'ah Manot

1. Each man and women must send a food gift composed of at least two types of food or drink that may be used for that day's festive meal to at least one person. The primary purpose of this mitzvah is to increase friendship between people. To some extent it may also provide for some needy.

2. It is praiseworthy to send *mishlo'ah manot* to many people and to send portions according to the standards of the giver, increasing harmony and amity in the nation.

3. At least the primary food gift that one sends to fulfill the mitzvah must be sent and received during the day of Purim.

4. The mitzvah is not fulfilled by sending money.

5. A mourner is required to fulfill the mitzvah of *mishlo'ah manot*. Others do not send to the mourner but may send to a spouse or other member of the family.

VI. Matanot La'ebyonim

1. In addition to *mishlo'ah manot*, during the day of Purim we must give food, substance or monetary gifts to at least two poor people or their representatives.

2. If one can afford it, it is appropriate to give to many more than the minimum two poor people or their representatives.

3. On Purim, we are not very particular with the recipients of charity – "Whosoever extends his hand, we give him."

VII. Se`udat Purim

1. Everyone must partake of a festive meal on Purim. This mitzvah is not fulfilled at night but only during the day.

2. As the miracle of Purim came about through festive banquets with drinking of wine, to some extent the Purim *se`uda* should have such a quality, including alcoholic beverages for the adults. The Talmud states that one should become so joyous until he does not know the difference between "Cursed is Haman, blessed is Mordekhai." Whatever interpretation is given to this statement, and there are many, it is absolutely clear that one may only drink to the extent that he does not violate a halakha and is able to recite birkat hamazon and relevant prayers with proper concentration.

VIII. Purim on Friday

The festive meal celebrating Purim is not to be held at night but at some point during the day. When Purim falls on a Friday, it is necessary to have the meal early enough in the day so as not to interfere with having the Friday night meal of Shabbat with appetite.

Some rabbis have advised having the meal in the morning. When impractical, the meal may be had in the early afternoon. For example, sunset on Purim day in the New York area (2008) is at 7:10 and the standard Friday minha-arbit services will begin at 6:40 for Shir Hashirim and 6:55 for minha. A festive meal beginning at 1 o'clock or 1:30 should allow enough time to have a Shabbat meal with appetite at 8 o'clock. (Those for whom it is practical may choose to pray with a minha gedola minyan at 1:05 p.m.).

Other rabbis have advised having the Purim meal attached to the Shabbat meal, essentially combining both into one great meal. In this option, the first part of the great meal is had shortly before Shabbat. Arbit should not be prayed beforehand. At candlelighting time, the women light the Shabbat candles and Shabbat is accepted by all, a covering is spread over the bread and Shabbat *qiddush* is recited. Assuming the berakha had already been said over the wine in the Purim portion of the meal, the *qiddush* is recited without the berakha on the wine. Assuming *hamosi* had already been said on bread in the Purim portion of the meal, that berakha also is not repeated in the Shabbat portion of the meal. In Birkat Hamazon, `al hanisim is recited for Purim and *reseh vehahalisenu* for Shabbat.

IX. Prayers

1. In the amida of Purim and in birkat hamazon we recite *Al Hanissim* followed by *Bimeh Mordekhai VeEsther* in their proper places as specified in all siddurim. If one forgot to recite them, he does not repeat the amida or birkat hamazon. If one remembered before having mentioned Hashem's name in the berakha following them, he may

Halakhot of Purim

"return" and say them at that spot and then proceed from there. One who remembered too late, but still is in the amida or birkat hamazon, should insert them at the end of the amida before *oseh shalom* or in the *harahman* portion of birkat hamazon.

2. Tefillin are donned on Purim.

3. Hallel is not recited on Purim. Some Talmudic sages say the megilla takes the place of Hallel. Others say Hallel is reserved for miracles that occur in the Land of Israel (subsequent to having originally entered the land). Others explain that we did not achieve freedom on Purim to be fully "servants of the Almighty," but remained under the rule of Ahashverosh in exile.

4. *Tahanunim* are not recited on Purim and Shushan Purim. There is no musaf on Purim.

5. Before arbit and in *shahrit* we recite Psalm 22. Here, the psalmist is in a grievous, life-threatening situation from his enemies and is ill from the troubles besetting him. He recalls G-d's saving intervention on behalf of the nation in the past and His caring for him from birth and is able to overcome his despair with prayer that obviously leads to salvation. The Sages applied this psalm to Haman's attempt to annihilate the Jewish People and Mordekhai and Esther's endeavors that brought salvation.

6. In arbit, the megilla is read after the amida followed by *ve'ata qadosh*. In *shahrit*, it is read after the Torah, just before *ve'ata qadosh*. (The verse of *ve'ata qadosh* is from the psalm we read on Purim (Psalm 22:4), and immediately follows the verse which the Talmud links to the halakha of reading the megilla by day and night.) On Saturday night,

163

the blessing *boreh me'oreh ha'esh* is recited before the reading.

7. There are three olim to the Torah on Purim. The portion read - from Parashat Beshalah - speaks of Joshua's battling and weakening Amaleq. It contains the famous scene of Moshe on the mountaintop. When his hand was raised Israel was ascendant, when lowered, Amaleq was ascendant. The Mishnah (R.H. 3:8) explains this as an allegory meaning that when Bene Yisrael turn their hearts to Hashem, they are successful, otherwise they are not.

X. General Halakhot

1. Purim is celebrated on Adar 14 in most of the world. In order to commemorate the one-day-later celebration of Shushan, where the battle continued for a second day, cities that were walled (like Shushan) when Joshua led the nation into the land of Israel (for example, Jerusalem) celebrate Purim on Adar 15.

2. It is prohibited to fast or have eulogies on Purim.

3. Public aspects of mourning are suspended for the day similarly to Shabbat. This is one of the cases where Shulhan Arukh codifies the halakha differently in two different chapters. We follow the later, lenient codification.

4. Working is permitted on Purim except in those places that have a specific custom not to work. In any event, doing business by buying and selling merchandise is permitted.

5. It is permitted to have weddings on Purim.

Index

165

Index

Index